SUPER EASY

Pasta!

SUPER EASY

Pasta!

Simple and Delicious Dinner Solutions

The Editors of
GOOD BOOKS

Good Books

New York, New York

Copyright © 2021 by Good Books
Photos by Claire Barboza, Bonnie Matthews, and Meredith Special Interest
Media. Photos on pages ii–xi courtesy of Shutterstock.

Good Books books may be purchased in bulk at special discounts for sales
promotion, corporate gifts, fund-raising, or educational purposes. Special editions
can also be created to specifications. For details, contact the Special Sales
Department, Good Books, 307 West 36th Street, 11th Floor, New York, NY 10018
or info@skyhorsepublishing.com.

Good Books is an imprint of Skyhorse Publishing, Inc.®, a Delaware corporation.

Visit our website at www.goodbooks.com.

10 9 8 7 6 5 4 3 2 1

Library of Congress Cataloging-in-Publication Data is available on file.

Cover design by Laura Klynstra
Cover photo courtesy of Meredith Special Interest Media

Print ISBN: 978-1-68099-757-6
Ebook ISBN: 978-1-68099-771-2

Printed in China

Contents

Getting Started

Pasta is one of the most versatile and universally appreciated foods. It's beloved by kids in the form of macaroni and cheese, spaghetti with marinara, or straight up with a pat of butter. It's perfect for date night at home (try Shrimp with Sun-Dried Tomatoes on page 92). Baked dishes like the Spinach Ravioli Bake on page 116 are perfect for a meal train or sharing at a potluck dinner. Comfort food favorites like Pasta à la Carbonara (page 66) are welcome on cold winter nights, while the Greek Pasta Salad (page 89) is ideal for a summer picnic. Pasta can be dressed up with freshly grated Parmesan and cracked pepper or dressed down with some Velveeta tossed in a slow cooker. This cookbook offers a wide range of easy-to-prepare pasta dishes so you're sure to find something for any occasion—including a last-minute Tuesday-night dinner with the kids. These recipes were collected from and tested by home cooks across the country, and their flavor profiles are just as diverse as the people who created them.

The one thing all the recipes have in common is that they're easy. Each recipe tells you the prep time required as well as the time needed for cooking or baking. Most recipes require 15 minutes or less of prep, and very few need more than 30 minutes. The cooking time varies according to the recipe and the appliance used. Ingredients used in this book shouldn't be hard to find in your local grocery store, and most are inexpensive, too. Although some recipes are simpler than others, none should stress you out. Just read the recipe all the way through before beginning to make sure you have all the ingredients (or have a plan to substitute for any you're missing) and to get a sense of where the recipe is going before you start. It's also helpful to do any prep work ahead of time—for example, veggies can be chopped and stored in the refrigerator in advance.

You'll see little icons on the top of each recipe that indicate whether the recipe is made using your stove, oven, slow cooker, or Instant Pot. You'll also see some recipes that are chilled, and some that require two appliances—perhaps the pasta is cooked on the stovetop and then thrown in the slow cooker with the other ingredients. If you're looking for a recipe made with a specific appliance, check the index. For example, under "Instant Pot," you'll find Insta Pasta à la Maria (page 29), Instant Pot Shells & Cheese with Kale (page 115), and more. Of course, slow-cooker recipes can also be made in an Instant Pot using the Slow Cook setting.

Beyond the appliances, you won't need many cooking tools. A big pot is good for cooking the pasta, and have a strainer handy for when the pasta is done. You'll want a wooden spoon for stirring the pasta and sauces and a sauté pan or skillet. A cheese grater is nice for finishing touches. Tongs or a pasta fork are helpful for serving. That's about it!

Freezing Sauces and Baked Pasta Dishes

The sauce recipes in this book (pages 1-12) can be made and frozen for future use. When you're done making the sauce, cool it completely, then ladle into plastic containers with secure, airtight lids or into airtight plastic freezer bags. Label with the name of the sauce and the date and use within three months. To use, transfer to the refrigerator to thaw completely, then heat in a skillet over low heat. For cream-based sauces, be sure to stir frequently as you're heating—it's likely that the sauce will have separated to some degree, so the stirring helps return the sauce to its original consistency.

Baked pasta dishes can also be frozen. Bake the dish in a disposable tin or use a pan you're not likely to need again anytime soon. Allow the pasta to cool completely. Cover tightly with a double layer of foil before freezing. Label with recipe name and date and use within three months. To reheat, you can transfer the pan directly from the freezer to the oven and bake at 350°F until heated through.

Choosing Pasta

Pasta Shapes

For most of the recipes in this book, a specific shape of pasta is recommended—linguine or penne or farfalle, for example. But with the exception of recipes like stuffed shells or ravioli that clearly require actual pasta shells or ravioli, feel free to substitute whatever shape of pasta you're in the mood for. There are over 500 pasta shapes to choose from, though you may only have a dozen or so represented in your local grocery store. Still, that's a lot of options to play around with. Just keep in mind that pasta shaped like scoops or with hollow centers or deep divots (think shells, penne, rotini) are better at holding thick or chunky sauces, while flat noodles (fettuccine, linguine, spaghetti) are better suited to thinner sauces.

Tagliatelle   Rotini   Penne Rigate   Farfalle

Pappardelle Festonate   Pipe Rigate

Conchiglie   Gramigna   Penne integrali   Orecchiette

Pasta Varieties

Most grocery stores carry pastas made from a variety of starches. You can likely find a wide variety of shapes made from semolina, which is derived from durum wheat. This is the most traditional kind of pasta, the delicious, satisfying, comforting pasta you're probably used to. But you may also find whole wheat pasta, a somewhat healthier alternative, as well as various gluten-free pastas, which may be made from rice flour, quinoa, amaranth, corn flour, or some combination of those. Gluten-free pastas have come a long way in the last decade and the flavor and texture of many options are truly satisfying, if not an exact replica of traditional pasta. More recently, a myriad of "alternative" pastas have shown up on shelves, too—pastas made from lentils, black beans, yellow peas, chickpeas, cassava, sweet potatoes, cauliflower, and more. Try them! Just remember that cooking time varies significantly between these kinds of pastas, so follow the instructions on the package they come in.

Cooking Pasta

There's no need to make cooking pasta complicated, but there are a few things you can do to make the process efficient and to ensure a delicious result. First, use a pot that's large enough—and fill it full enough with water—for the pasta to move freely in the water. You don't want the noodles to be cramped. Use about 4 quarts of water per pound of pasta. Second, allow the water to come to a full rolling boil (keep a lid on to speed this up), and then add about 1 tablespoon of salt per 4 quarts of pasta/one pound of pasta. Salted water takes longer to boil, so don't add the salt until the water is already boiling. Some people like to put a glug of olive oil in the water to help prevent the pasta from sticking together. However, this also makes the pasta slippery, which means sauce won't cling to it as well. When the salted water is boiling rapidly, add the pasta and give it a stir so that it doesn't clump together. Stir periodically until the pasta is fully cooked. Check the pasta package to see how long to cook the pasta and set a timer for the shortest time period if you're likely to lose track. Use a spoon or tongs to remove a piece of pasta from the water, allow it to cool a few seconds, and then bite into it to see if it's done enough. For al dente ("to the tooth" in Italian) pasta, you want the pasta a bit chewy, but there shouldn't be any crunch. However, remember that if you're going to be putting the pasta in a slow cooker or in the oven for more cooking time, err slightly on the side of underdone pasta to avoid the pasta turning to mush in the next steps.

When the pasta is almost done, make sure you have a colander ready in the sink. Before you drain the pasta, notice if the recipe calls for a scoop or two of pasta water. Often, adding some pasta water to the sauce aids its consistency.

Don't let the pasta sit in its water any longer than absolutely necessary. Pour into the colander to drain thoroughly, then return drained pasta to its pot and cover to keep warm, if desired.

Time to dive into the recipes!

For many recipes in this book, you can get the sauce started while you're boiling the pasta water or cooking the pasta. You may want to have the pasta pot on a back burner, because you're likely to need to stir the sauce more often than you'll need to stir the pasta.

Sauces

Fresh Tomato Spaghetti Sauce

Beverly Hummel,
Fleetwood, PA

Makes 12 cups
Prep. Time: 20 minutes
Cooking/Baking Time: 4–5 hours
Ideal slow-cooker size: 6-qt.

4 quarts cherry tomatoes

1 onion, minced

2 garlic cloves, minced

1 tablespoon oil

3 teaspoons sugar

3 teaspoons fresh chopped rosemary

2 tablespoons fresh chopped thyme and/or basil

2 teaspoons Italian seasoning

1 teaspoon salt

½ teaspoon pepper

1. Stem tomatoes, leaving the skins on. Blend until smooth in blender.

2. In a skillet, sauté onion and garlic in oil.

3. Add the onion and garlic to slow cooker. Add tomatoes, sugar, rosemary, thyme, Italian seasoning, salt, and pepper.

4. Simmer on Low in slow cooker until thickened, about 4 to 5 hours. Remove the lid for the final 30 to 60 minutes of cooking time if you'd like a thicker sauce.

Meat Sauce for a Crowd

Becky Fixel,
Grosse Pointe Farms, MI

Makes 45–50 servings
Prep. Time: 20 minutes
Cooking/Baking Time: 8 hours
Ideal slow-cooker size: 7-qt.

2 tablespoons olive oil

28-ounce can crushed tomatoes

28-ounce can tomato sauce

15-ounce can Italian stewed tomatoes

6-ounce can tomato paste

2–3 tablespoons basil

2 tablespoons oregano

2 tablespoons brown sugar

2 tablespoons garlic paste (or 2 medium cloves, peeled and minced)

2 lb. extra-lean ground sirloin or lean ground turkey

1. Pour olive oil in the crock. Use a paper towel to rub it all around the inside.

2. Add all ingredients except ground sirloin. Stir together and put slow cooker on Low.

3. In a large skillet, brown ground sirloin, draining off any extra grease. Add this to slow cooker.

4. Cook on Low for 8 hours.

TIP

This recipe makes enough for a big crowd or for several meals. Freeze extra sauce or can it for later!

Classic Pesto

**Leona Yoder,
Hartville, OH**

Makes about 1½ cups
Prep. Time: 10 minutes

2 cups lightly packed fresh basil

1 cup (about 5 ounces) grated Parmesan cheese

½–⅔ cup extra-virgin olive oil, divided

1–2 garlic cloves, optional

1. In a blender or food processor, blend basil, Parmesan, ½ the olive oil, and garlic (if using) until smooth. Add more oil until desired consistency is achieved.

2. If you're not ready to use the pesto immediately, cover and refrigerate it for up to 5 days, or freeze it if you want to store it longer.

Spinach Pesto

**Vic and Christina Buckwalter,
Keezletown, VA**

Makes 1½ cups pesto
Prep. Time: 15 minutes
Cooking/Baking Time: 12 minutes

4 packed cups fresh spinach leaves

3 garlic cloves

2 tablespoons pine nuts

¼ packed cup fresh basil

½ cup extra-virgin olive oil

⅛ teaspoon salt

1. Process all ingredients in blender until smooth. Store in refrigerator or freeze for later use.

TIP

When ready to use, cook 1 pound linguine according to package directions. Drain, saving 2 tablespoons of pasta water. Mix together ¼–½ cup of pesto, a few tablespoons of freshly grated Parmesan cheese, and reserved pasta water. Stir mixture into pasta.

Southwestern Pesto

**Carrie Wood,
Paxton, MA**

Makes 4–6 servings
Prep. Time: 10 minutes
Cooking/Baking Time: 10–12 minutes

1 cup loosely packed cilantro leaves

1 cup loosely packed flat parsley

⅓ cup toasted pepitas (pumpkin seeds)

1 garlic clove, peeled

½ cup crumbled feta cheese

½ cup extra-virgin olive oil

salt to taste

1. Process all ingredients in a food processor until a rough paste is formed, adding additional olive oil if the paste seems too dry.

Cauliflower Vegan Alfredo

**Sue Hamilton,
Benson, AZ**

Makes 4 servings
Prep. Time: 5 minutes
Cooking/Baking Time: 6 hours
Ideal slow-cooker size: 3-qt.

1-pound bag frozen cauliflower

13.5-ounce can light coconut milk

½ cup diced onion

2 garlic cloves, minced

1 tablespoon vegetable stock concentrate

Salt, to taste

Pepper, to taste

1. Place frozen cauliflower, coconut milk, onion, garlic, and vegetable stock concentrate in slow-cooker crock. Stir mixture to blend in the stock concentrate.

2. Cover and cook on Low for 6 hours.

3. Place cooked mixture in blender and process until smooth.

4. Add salt and pepper to taste.

Alfredo Sauce

**Barbara Kuhns,
Millersburg, OH**

Makes 2½–3 cups
Prep. Time: 3–5 minutes
Cooking/Baking Time: 20 minutes

1 stick (8 tablespoons) butter

1 pint heavy cream

1 teaspoon garlic powder

Pepper, optional

½ cup Parmesan cheese

2 tablespoons cream cheese, softened

1. In small saucepan, lightly brown butter.

2. Add rest of ingredients and simmer over low heat for 15 minutes, or until all ingredients are well blended. Stir occasionally to prevent sticking and scorching.

Pasta with Chicken

Chicken Tomato Pasta

**Gwendolyn Muholland,
Corryton, TN**

Makes 6 servings
Prep. Time: 10 minutes
Cooking/Baking Time: 4–8 hours

2–3 boneless, skinless chicken breasts

1 bell pepper, chopped

1 small onion, chopped

23.5-ounce jar traditional Italian tomato pasta
sauce (or 3 cups homemade sauce, page 3)

14.5-ounce jar Alfredo sauce (or 1¾ cups
homemade Alfredo Sauce, page 12)

1 cup shredded mozzarella cheese

16-ounce box rotini pasta

1. Place uncooked chicken breasts in bottom of slow cooker. Add pepper and onion.

2. Top with Italian tomato pasta sauce, Alfredo sauce, and shredded mozzarella.

3. Cover and cook on Low for 6 to 8 hours or High for 4 hours.

4. When you're ready to eat, cook pasta according to instructions on package.

5. Serve chicken on top of pasta with sauce.

Creamy Parmesan Chicken and Linguine

**Orpha Herr,
Andover, NY**

Makes 8 servings
Prep. Time: 15–20 minutes
Cooking/Baking Time: 4–10 hours
Ideal slow-cooker size: 5-qt.

8 boneless, skinless chicken breast halves

1 teaspoon fresh lemon juice

Salt, to taste

Pepper, to taste

2 (10.75-ounce) cans cream of celery soup

⅓ cup sherry or wine, optional

¼ cup grated Parmesan cheese

16-ounce box linguine

1. Rinse chicken breasts and pat dry. Place chicken in slow cooker in layers. Season each layer with a sprinkling of lemon juice, salt, and pepper.

2. In a medium bowl, mix soups with sherry or wine, if using. Pour mixture over chicken. Sprinkle with Parmesan cheese.

3. Cover and cook on Low for 8 to 10 hours, or on High for 4 to 5 hours, or until chicken is tender but not dry or mushy.

4. Cook linguine according to instructions on the package.

5. Use tongs to place pasta on each plate or bowl and then scoop a piece of chicken and sauce over top.

Pasta with Chicken, Tomatoes, and Olives

**Diane Clement,
Rogers, AR**

Makes 6–8 servings
Prep. Time: 30 minutes
Cooking/Baking Time: 3 hours
Ideal slow-cooker size: 5- or 6-qt.

2 cups cooked chopped chicken

1½ cups chopped onion

1 teaspoon minced garlic

3 (28-ounce) cans Italian plum tomatoes, drained

2 teaspoons dried basil

¼–½ teaspoon red pepper flakes, according to the amount of heat you like

2 cups chicken broth

Salt, to taste

Pepper, to taste

3 tablespoons olive oil

1 pound penne or rigatoni

2½ cups Havarti cheese cubes

⅓ cup sliced, pitted, brine-cured olives (such as kalamata olives)

⅓ cup grated Parmesan cheese

¼ cup finely chopped fresh basil

1. Grease interior of slow-cooker crock.

2. Place chicken, onion, garlic, tomatoes, dried basil, and red pepper flakes in crock. Stir together well, breaking up tomatoes with back of spoon.

3. Stir in chicken broth.

4. Season with salt and pepper.

5. Cover. Cook on High for 2 hours.

6. Cook pasta according to instructions on package.

7. In slow-cooker crock or in a large bowl, toss pasta together with the sauce and remaining ingredients and serve.

Chicken Broccoli Alfredo

**Mahlon Miller,
Hutchinson, KS**

Makes 4 servings
Prep. Time: 30 minutes
Cooking/Baking Time: 1–2 hours
Ideal slow-cooker size: 3-qt.

8 ounces fettuccine

1½ cups fresh or frozen broccoli

2 cups cooked cubed chicken

10.75-ounce can cream of mushroom soup

½ cup grated mild cheddar cheese

1. Cook noodles according to instructions on package, adding broccoli during the last 4 minutes of cooking time. Drain.

2. In slow cooker, combine all ingredients.

3. Cover and cook on Low for 1 to 2 hours, or until heated through and until cheese is melted.

TIP

This is a great recipe for using up leftover rotisserie or baked chicken. Or you can purchase precooked chicken breasts. Of course, you can also poach, grill, or bake raw skinless chicken breasts and cut them up in small pieces before adding to the crock.

That's Amore Chicken Cacciatore

**Carol Sherwood,
Batavia, NY**

Makes 6 servings
Prep. Time: 20 minutes
Cooking/Baking Time: 7–9 hours
Ideal slow-cooker size: 6-qt.

6 boneless, skinless chicken breast halves, divided

28-ounce jar spaghetti sauce or 3½ cups homemade tomato sauce (page 3)

2 green bell peppers, chopped

1 onion, minced

2 tablespoons minced garlic

16-ounce box farfalle

1. Place a layer of chicken in slow cooker.

2. In bowl, combine remaining ingredients. Spoon ½ of sauce over first layer of chicken.

3. Add remaining breast halves. Top with remaining sauce.

4. Cover and cook on Low for 7 to 9 hours, or until chicken is tender but not dry.

5. Cook farfalle according to instructions on package.

6. Use tongs to place pasta on each plate, then add a chicken breast and sauce.

Ann's Chicken Cacciatore

**Ann Driscoll,
Albuquerque, NM**

Makes 6–8 servings
Prep. Time: 10 minutes
Cooking/Baking Time: 3–9 hours
Ideal slow-cooker size: 4-qt.

1 large onion, thinly sliced

2½–3-pound chicken, cut up

2 (6-ounce) cans tomato paste

4-ounce can sliced mushrooms, drained

1 teaspoon salt

¼ cup dry white wine

¼ teaspoon pepper

1–2 garlic cloves, minced

1–2 teaspoons dried oregano

½ teaspoon dried basil

½ teaspoon celery seed, optional

1 bay leaf

16-ounce box spaghetti

1. Place onion in slow-cooker crock. Add chicken.

2. Combine remaining ingredients except spaghetti. Pour over chicken.

3. Cover. Cook on Low for 7 to 9 hours, or on High for 3 to 4 hours.

4. Prepare spaghetti according to instructions on package. Drain and serve with chicken and sauce.

Ground Turkey Cacciatore Spaghetti

**Maria Shevlin,
Sicklerville, NJ**

Makes 6–8 servings
Prep. Time: 15–20 minutes
Cooking/Baking Time: 5 minutes
Setting: Sauté and Manual
Pressure: High
Release: Manual

1 teaspoon olive oil

1 medium sweet onion, chopped

3 garlic cloves, minced

1 pound ground turkey

32-ounce jar spaghetti sauce or
    1 quart homemade sauce (page 3)

1 teaspoon salt

½ teaspoon black pepper

½ teaspoon oregano

½ teaspoon dried basil

½ teaspoon red pepper flakes

1 cup bell pepper strips, mixed colors if desired

1 cup diced mushrooms

16-ounce box spaghetti

3 cups chicken bone broth

1. Press Sauté button on the Instant Pot and add oil, onion, and garlic to inner pot.

2. Add ground turkey and break it up a little while it browns.

3. Once ground turkey is browned, add sauce and seasonings.

4. Add bell peppers and mushrooms and stir.

5. Add spaghetti—break it in half in order for it to fit in.

6. Add chicken bone broth.

7. Lock lid, make sure vent is at sealing, and set on Manual at high pressure for 6 minutes.

8. When cook time is up, manually release the pressure.

SERVING SUGGESTION

Top with some fresh grated Parmesan cheese and basil.

Cheesy Buffalo Chicken Pasta

Christina Gerber
Apple Creek, OH

Makes 6–8 servings
Prep. Time: 15 minutes
Cooking/Baking Time: 4½–5 hours
Ideal slow-cooker size: 6-qt.

3 cups chicken broth

½ cup Buffalo wing sauce, divided

1 tablespoon dry ranch dressing mix

¾ teaspoon garlic powder

½ teaspoon salt

⅛ teaspoon black pepper

1½ lb. boneless, skinless chicken thighs

8-ounce package cream cheese, cubed

1 cup shredded sharp cheddar cheese

1 tablespoon cornstarch

1 tablespoon water

1 pound linguine

Chopped cilantro, optional

1. Grease interior of slow-cooker crock.

2. In crock, combine broth, ¼ cup Buffalo sauce, and seasonings.

3. Submerge chicken in sauce.

4. Scatter cubed cream cheese and shredded cheese over chicken.

5. Cover. Cook on Low for 4 hours, or until instant-read thermometer registers 160°–165°F when stuck in thighs.

6. When chicken is fully cooked, remove to bowl and shred with 2 forks. (Cover crock to keep sauce warm.)

7. Add remaining ¼ cup Buffalo sauce to shredded chicken and toss to coat. Set aside but keep warm.

8. In small bowl, stir cornstarch and water together until smooth. Stir into warm sauce in crock until sauce becomes smooth and thick.

9. Break noodles in half and place in crock.

10. Top with shredded chicken and cover.

11. Cook on High for 30 to 60 minutes, or just until noodles are fully cooked. Stir 3 or 4 times during cooking.

12. If you need more liquid for noodles to cook, add water ¼ cup at a time.

13. Garnish with cilantro, if using, and serve immediately.

Super Easy Pasta!

Insta Pasta à la Maria

Maria Shevlin
Sicklerville, NJ

Makes 6–8 servings
Prep. Time: 10–15 minutes
Cooking/Baking Time: 6 minutes
Setting: Manual
Pressure: High
Release: Manual

32-ounce jar of your favorite spaghetti sauce or
   1 quart of homemade sauce (page 3)

2 cups fresh chopped spinach

1 cup chopped mushrooms

½ precooked shredded rotisserie chicken

1 teaspoon salt

½ teaspoon black pepper

½ teaspoon dried basil

¼ teaspoon red pepper flakes

1 teaspoon parsley flakes

13.25 ounces pasta, any shape or brand

3 cups water

1. Place sauce in the bottom of inner pot of Instant Pot.

2. Add spinach, then mushrooms.

3. Add chicken on top of vegetables and sauce.

4. Add seasonings and stir.

5. Add pasta.

6. Add 3 cups of water.

7. Secure lid and move vent to sealing. Set to Manual on high pressure for 6 minutes.

8. When cook time is up, release pressure manually.

9. Remove lid and stir.

Angel Chicken Pasta

Makes 4 servings
Prep Time: 10 minutes
Cooking/Baking Time: 5–6 hours
Ideal slow-cooker size: 4- to 5-qt.

¼ cup butter

.7-ounce envelope dry Italian salad dressing mix

½ cup dry white wine

10.75-ounce can golden mushroom soup

½ (8-ounce) container cream cheese with chives

4 boneless, skinless chicken breast halves

8 ounces angel-hair pasta

1. In large saucepan over low heat, melt butter. Stir in salad dressing mix. Add wine and soup, stirring to blend. Add cream cheese and stir until smooth. Do not boil.

2. Arrange chicken in slow cooker. Pour sauce over top.

3. Cover and cook on Low for 5 to 6 hours or just until chicken is tender but not dry.

4. Prepare pasta according to the instructions on package. Drain and serve with the chicken and sauce.

STOVETOP

Skinny Chicken Stroganoff

**Carol Sherwood,
Batavia, NY**

Makes 6 servings
Prep. Time: 10–15 minutes
Cooking/Baking Time: 20–25 minutes

4 slices turkey bacon

6 ounces whole wheat noodles

¾ cup reduced-fat sour cream

¼ cup all-purpose flour

14.5-ounce can low-fat, low-sodium chicken broth

⅛ teaspoon black pepper

1 pound boneless, skinless chicken breasts, cut into ¼-inch strips

8 ounces sliced fresh mushrooms

1 cup chopped onion

1 garlic clove, pressed

2 tablespoons snipped fresh parsley

1. In large skillet, cook bacon until crisp. Remove from pan, break, and set aside.

2. Cook noodles according to instructions on package. Drain and keep warm.

3. In a large bowl, whisk together sour cream and flour until smooth.

4. Gradually whisk in chicken broth until smooth. Stir in pepper. Set aside.

5. Heat skillet that you used for bacon over high heat until hot. Add chicken. Cook, stirring continually for 3 minutes, or until meat is no longer pink. Remove from pan and set aside. Keep warm.

6. Reduce heat to medium. Add mushrooms, onion, and garlic. Cook and stir 3 minutes.

7. Stir in chicken and bacon.

8. Stir in sour cream mixture. Bring to a boil.

9. Reduce heat. Simmer for 2 minutes, stirring constantly.

10. Remove from heat. Stir in parsley.

11. Serve over prepared noodles.

Slow Cooker Chicken Stroganoff

Brenda Pope,
Dundee, OH

Makes 4 servings
Prep. Time: 5 minutes
Cooking/Baking Time: 8 hours
Ideal slow-cooker size: 4-qt.

1 pound boneless, skinless chicken breasts

.87-ounce package dry chicken gravy mix

10.75-ounce can cream of mushroom or chicken soup

1 cup white wine

8-ounce package cream cheese, softened

8 ounces egg noodles

1. Put chicken in slow cooker. Sprinkle gravy mix on top. In separate bowl, combine soup and wine and pour over gravy mix.

2. Cover. Cook on Low for 8 hours.

3. During last 30 minutes of cooking time, stir in cream cheese. Before serving, remove chicken (keeping it warm) and whisk the sauce until smooth.

4. Prepare noodles according to instructions on package. Drain and serve with the sauce.

Chicken Marengo

**Marcia Parker,
Lansdale, PA**

Makes 4–5 servings
Prep Time: 5–10 minutes
Cooking/Baking Time: 6–7 hours
Ideal slow-cooker size: 6-qt.

2.5-3-pound frying chicken, cut up and skinned

2 envelopes dry spaghetti sauce mix

½ cup dry white wine

2 fresh tomatoes, quartered

¼ pound fresh mushrooms

8-10 ounces linguine

1. Place chicken pieces in the bottom of slow cooker.

2. In small bowl, combine dry spaghetti sauce mix with wine. Pour it over chicken.

3. Cover and cook on Low for 5½ to 6½ hours.

4. Turn temperature to High and add tomatoes and mushrooms.

5. Cover and cook on High for 30 to 40 minutes or until vegetables are hot.

6. Prepare the linguine according to instructions on package. Drain and serve with chicken and sauce.

Italian Chicken

**Starla Kreider,
Mohrsville, PA**

Makes 4 servings
Prep Time: 5 minutes
Cooking/Baking Time: 2½–8 hours
Ideal slow-cooker size: 3-qt.

4 boneless, skinless chicken breast halves

28-ounce jar spaghetti sauce, your choice of special seasonings and ingredients

4 ounces shredded mozzarella cheese

8–10 ounces fettuccine or tagliatelle

1. Place chicken in slow cooker.

2. Pour spaghetti sauce over chicken.

3. Cover and cook on High for 2½ to 3½ hours, or on for Low 6 to 8 hours

4. Place chicken on serving platter and sprinkle with cheese.

5. Prepare pasta according to instructions on package. Drain and serve with the chicken and sauce.

Super Easy Pasta!

Easy Tomato-Alfredo Chicken

**Gwendolyn Muholland,
Corryton, TN**

Makes 4–6 servings
Prep. Time: 5–20 minutes
Cooking/Baking Time: 4–8 hours
Ideal slow-cooker size: 4-qt.

2–3 boneless, skinless chicken breasts

23.5-ounce jar Prego Traditional Italian sauce or 2¾ cups homemade tomato sauce (page 3)

14.5-ounce jar Prego Homestyle Alfredo sauce or 1¾ cups homemade Alfredo Sauce (page 12)

1 cup shredded mozzarella cheese

16-ounce box rigatoni

1. Place uncooked chicken breasts in the bottom of slow cooker.

2. Top with Italian sauce, Alfredo sauce, and shredded mozzarella.

3. Cover and cook on Low for 6 to 8 hours or High for 4 hours.

4. When you're ready to eat, cook pasta according to instructions on package. Drain.

5. Serve chicken on top of pasta with sauce.

Balsamic Chicken

Hope Comerford,
Clinton Township, MI

Makes 4 servings
Prep. Time: 10 minutes
Cooking/Baking Time: 5–6 hours
Ideal slow-cooker size: 3-qt.

2 pounds boneless, skinless chicken breasts

2 tablespoons olive oil

½ teaspoon salt

½ teaspoon pepper

1 onion, halved and sliced

28-ounce can diced tomatoes

½ cup balsamic vinegar

2 teaspoons sugar

2 teaspoons garlic powder

2 teaspoons Italian seasoning

8 ounces fusilli

1. Place chicken in crock. Drizzle with olive oil and sprinkle with salt and pepper.

2. Spread the onion over the top of the chicken.

3. In bowl, mix together the diced tomatoes, balsamic vinegar, sugar, garlic powder, and Italian seasoning. Pour this over chicken and onions.

4. Cover and cook on Low for 5 to 6 hours.

5. Cook pasta according to instructions on package. Drain pasta and serve with chicken over top.

Thai Chicken and Noodles

**Vonnie Oyer,
Hubbard, OR**

Makes 4 servings
Prep. Time: 15 minutes
Cooking/Baking Time: 30 minutes
Setting: Manual then Slow Cook
Pressure: High
Release: Manual

Thai peanut sauce:

¾ cup light coconut milk

½ cup peanut butter

2 tablespoons sesame oil

¼ cup fresh lime juice

2 tablespoons soy sauce

1½ teaspoons crushed red pepper flakes

1 tablespoon seasoned rice vinegar

1 tablespoon honey

¼ teaspoon ground ginger

Chicken:

1.5 lb. boneless, skinless chicken breasts

1½ cups chicken broth

8 ounces dry rice noodles

5 ounces sugar snap peas (about 1½ cups)

1. In a blender, mix sauce ingredients. Makes 2 cups (this recipe uses 1 cup).

2. To inner pot of the Instant Pot, add chicken, 1 cup Thai peanut sauce, and broth.

3. Secure lid and make sure vent is at sealing. Cook on Manual at high pressure for 12 minutes.

4. Do a quick release (manual) of the pressure. Remove chicken from pot, leaving the sauce.

5. To sauce, add noodles and ensure all dry noodles are submerged in sauce. Top with peas and replace cover as quickly as possible.

6. Change setting to Slow Cook and cook for 10 minutes, or until noodles are soft but firm.

7. Meanwhile, shred chicken breasts and set aside.

8. When cook time is up, remove lid of Instant Pot and stir noodles. Stir chicken back into the inner pot with noodles.

Creamy Chicken Italiano

Sharon Easter,
Yuba City, CA
Rebecca Meyerkorth,
Wamego, KS
Bonnie Miller,
Cochranville, PA

Makes 4 servings
Prep. Time: 5 minutes
Cooking/Baking Time: 4 hours
Ideal slow-cooker size: 4-qt.

4 boneless, skinless chicken breast halves

1 envelope dry Italian salad dressing mix

¼ cup water

8-ounce package cream cheese, softened

10.75-ounce can cream of chicken soup

4-ounce can mushroom stems and pieces, drained

8 ounces fettuccine

1. Place chicken in slow cooker.

2. Combine salad dressing mix and water. Pour over chicken.

3. Cover. Cook on Low for 3 hours.

4. Combine cheese and soup until blended. Stir in mushrooms. Pour over chicken.

5. Cover. Cook on Low for 1 hour, or until chicken juices run clear.

6. Cook pasta according to instructions on package. Drain pasta and serve with chicken and sauce.

Chicken and Egg Noodles

**Janie Steele,
Moore, OK**

Makes 5–7 servings
Prep. Time: 15 minutes
Cooking/Baking Time: 5–6 hours
Ideal slow-cooker size: 5-qt.

14-ounce can low-sodium cream of chicken soup

2 (15.5-ounce) cans low-sodium chicken broth

1 teaspoon garlic powder

1 teaspoon onion powder

¼ teaspoon celery seed

¼ teaspoon pepper

4 tablespoons butter or margarine

1 pound boneless, skinless chicken breasts

24-ounce bag frozen egg noodles

1. Place all ingredients in crock except the noodles.

2. Cover and cook on Low for 5 to 6 hours.

3. Remove chicken and shred. Return to slow cooker, then add frozen noodles and cook for an additional 40 to 60 minutes, or until noodles are tender.

Creamy Chicken and Noodles

**Rhonda Burgoon,
Collingswood, NJ**

Makes 6 servings

Prep. Time: 25 minutes

Cooking/Baking Time: 4¼ –9¼ hours

Ideal slow-cooker size: 4-qt.

2 cups sliced carrots

1½ cups chopped onions

1 cup sliced celery

2 tablespoons snipped fresh parsley

1 bay leaf

3 medium chicken legs and thighs (about 2 lb.), skin removed

2 (10.75-ounce) cans 98%-fat-free, reduced-sodium cream of chicken soup

½ cup water

1 teaspoon dried thyme

¼ teaspoon salt

¼ teaspoon pepper

1 cup frozen peas

8 ounces fettuccine

SERVING SUGGESTION

Serve with crusty bread and a salad.

1. Place carrots, onions, celery, parsley, and bay leaf in bottom of slow cooker.

2. Place chicken on top of vegetables.

3. Combine soup, water, thyme, salt, and pepper. Pour over chicken and vegetables.

4. Cover. Cook on Low for 8 to 9 hours or on High for 4 to 4½ hours.

5. Remove chicken from slow cooker. Cool slightly. Remove from bones, cut into bite-size pieces, and return to slow cooker.

6. Remove and discard bay leaf.

7. Stir peas into mixture in slow cooker. Allow to cook for 5 to 10 more minutes.

8. Prepare pasta according to instructions on package. Drain and serve with the chicken and sauce.

Gnocchi with Chicken

**Janie Steele,
Moore, OK**

Makes 8 servings
Prep. Time: 30 minutes
Cooking/Baking Time: 7 hours
Ideal slow-cooker size: 5-qt.

1 pound gnocchi, store-bought or homemade

2 cups cooked chicken, cut into cubes

1 onion, chopped

1 cup chopped or shredded carrots

2 garlic cloves

Salt, to taste

Pepper, to taste

2 cups heavy cream

1½ cups grated Parmesan cheese

¼ teaspoon nutmeg

1½ cups fresh chopped spinach

1. Cook gnocchi according to instructions on package. Drain and add gnocchi and other ingredients except spinach to slow cooker.

2. Cover and cook on Low for 7 hours. Add spinach during the last 30 minutes and serve.

Pasta with Ham or Beef

Pork Tenderloin with Pasta in Tomato and Red Pepper Sauce

**Joyce Clark,
East Amherst, NY**

Makes 4–6 servings
Prep. Time: 15 minutes
Cooking/Baking Time: 30 minutes

1 tablespoon butter

1 tablespoon vegetable oil

2 cups sliced mushrooms

2 onions, chopped

2 garlic cloves, crushed

1 red bell pepper, chopped

3 teaspoons fresh chopped oregano

2 tablespoons flour

1 teaspoon chili powder

½ teaspoon salt

½ teaspoon black pepper

1 pound pork tenderloin, cut into 1" cubes

3 cups milk

9 ounces dry penne pasta

14-ounce can tomato sauce

1. In large skillet, melt butter. Add vegetable oil, mushrooms, onions, garlic, red pepper, and oregano. Cook over medium heat until onion is softened.

2. Place flour, chili powder, salt, and pepper in a ziplock plastic bag. Add pork pieces and shake to coat.

3. Add floured pork and any remaining flour mixture to skillet. Cook, stirring occasionally, until pork is browned on all sides.

4. Add milk, pasta, and tomato sauce. Bring mixture to a boil, stirring constantly.

5. Reduce heat, cover, and simmer for 15 minutes until pasta is tender.

Zesty Pasta

Carol Collins,
Holly Springs, NC

Makes 8 servings
Prep. Time: 10 minutes
Cooking/Baking Time: 1¾–2¼ hours

½ tablespoon olive oil

1½ cups chopped onions

1 pound 95%-lean ground sirloin or bison

3 garlic cloves, minced

2 teaspoons black pepper

1 teaspoon dried oregano

28-ounce can tomato purée, no salt added

15-ounce can tomato sauce, no salt added

½ teaspoon sugar, optional

1 pound whole wheat pasta

1. Heat olive oil in large stockpot over medium heat. Add onions and sauté until golden. Remove onions with slotted spoon and reserve.

2. Add ground meat and garlic to stockpot. Cook until meat is browned and no longer pink inside.

3. Add reserved onions, black pepper, oregano, tomato purée, and tomato sauce. Cook over low heat, partially covered, for 1½ hours.

4. Stir occasionally. Add water by ¼ cupfuls if sauce appears too thick.

5. Adjust taste with sugar, if using.

6. Cook pasta according to instructions on package. Drain and top with pasta sauce.

TIP

1. If preparing this recipe for young children, reduce black pepper to 1 teaspoon.
2. Serve this sauce over hearty pasta like thick spaghetti or cavatappi (spiral hollow noodles).
3. Use leftover sauce as a topping for pizza.

Creamy Spirals with Beef

Janet Oberholtzer,
Ephrata, PA
Renee Baum,
Chambersburg, PA

Makes 10–12 servings
Prep. Time: 30 minutes
Cooking/Baking Time: 2–2½ hours
Ideal slow-cooker size: 4- to 5-qt.

1 pound spiral pasta

¾ stick (6 tablespoons) butter

2 cups half-and-half

10.75-ounce can cheddar cheese soup

1½ cups leftover shredded beef

2–4 cups shredded cheddar cheese, depending upon how creamy you'd like the dish to be

1. Cook pasta according to instructions on package, being careful not to overcook it. Drain.

2. Return pasta to saucepan. Stir in butter until it melts.

3. Combine half-and-half and soup in slow cooker, blending well.

4. Stir pasta, leftover shredded beef, and shredded cheese into mixture in cooker.

5. Cover and cook on Low for 2 to 2½ hours, or until heated through and until cheese melts. (If you're home, stir the dish at the end of the first hour of cooking.)

Bow-Tie Pasta with Peas and Bacon

**J. B. Miller,
Indianapolis, IN**

Makes 4 servings
Prep Time: 5 minutes
Cooking/Baking Time: 20 minutes

16-ounce package farfalle (bow-tie pasta)

3 strips bacon

2–3 ounces blue cheese

2 cups frozen peas

Salt, to taste

Pepper, to taste

1. Cook pasta in boiling, salted water according to instructions on package.

2. While pasta cooks, dice bacon and crumble cheese.

3. In large skillet, cook bacon over medium-high heat until crisp. Remove and drain bacon, keeping 1 tablespoon of pan drippings.

4. When pasta is done but before draining it, stir frozen peas into pasta cooking water. Drain well and place in large bowl.

5. Add bacon, cheese, and reserved pan drippings to pasta and peas. Toss.

6. Add salt and freshly ground pepper to taste. Mix well and serve.

Cheese Tortellini and Meatballs with Vodka Pasta Sauce

**Phyllis Good,
Lancaster, PA**

Makes 4–6 servings
Prep Time: 10 minutes
Cooking/Baking Time: 6 hours
Ideal slow-cooker size: 5-qt.

1.5-pound bag frozen cheese tortellini

1.5-pound bag frozen Italian-style meatballs

20-ounce jar vodka pasta sauce

8-ounce can tomato sauce

1 cup water

1½ teaspoons dried oregano

1½ teaspoons dried basil

½ teaspoon dried crushed red pepper, or less if desired

2 cups shredded mozzarella cheese

Fresh basil, for garnish

1. In greased slow cooker, combine all ingredients except cheese and basil.

2. Cover and cook on Low for 6 hours.

3. Top each serving with shredded cheese. Garnish, if desired.

Hungarian Goulash

**Audrey Romonosky,
Austin, TX**

Makes 6 servings
Prep. Time: 20 minutes
Cooking/Baking Time: 8¼ hours
Ideal slow-cooker size: 4-qt.

2 lb. beef chuck, cubed, trimmed of fat

1 medium onion, sliced

½ teaspoon garlic powder

½ cup ketchup

2 tablespoons Worcestershire sauce

1 tablespoon brown sugar

¼ teaspoon salt

2 teaspoons paprika

½ teaspoon dry mustard

1 cup cold water

¼ cup flour

½ cup room-temperature water

12 ounces egg noodles

1. Place meat in slow cooker. Add onion.

2. Combine garlic powder, ketchup, Worcestershire sauce, brown sugar, salt, paprika, mustard, and cold water. Pour over meat.

3. Cover. Cook on Low for 8 hours.

4. Dissolve flour in room-temperature water. Stir into meat mixture. Cook on High until thickened, about 10 minutes.

5. Cook egg noodles according to instructions on package. Serve with sauce.

Sausage Tortellini

Christie Detamore-Hunsberger,
Harrisonburg, VA

Makes 8 servings
Prep. Time: 25–30 minutes
Cooking/Baking Time: 1½–2½ hours
Ideal slow-cooker size: 6-qt.

1½ cups sliced chicken sausage

1 tablespoon olive oil

1 cup chopped onions

2 garlic cloves, minced

5 cups beef or chicken broth

¾ cup water

¾ cup red wine

2 (14.75-ounce) cans diced tomatoes, undrained

1 cup thinly sliced carrots

¾ teaspoon dried basil

¾ teaspoon dried oregano

16-ounce can tomato sauce

¾ cup sliced zucchini, optional

16-ounce package tortellini

3 tablespoons chopped fresh parsley

1. Sauté sliced chicken sausage in olive oil until cooked through and browned.

2. Add sausage, onions, garlic, broth, water, wine, tomatoes and their juices, carrots, basil, oregano, and tomato sauce to crock. Stir together well.

3. Add zucchini, if using, and tortellini.

4. Cover. Cook on High for 1½ to 2½ hours, or until pasta is as tender as you like it, but not mushy.

5. Stir in parsley and serve.

Spaghetti Salad

**Lois Stoltzfus,
Honey Brook, PA**

Makes 6–8 servings
Prep. Time: 15 minutes
Cooking/Baking Time: 15 minutes
Cooling Time: 30 minutes

16-ounce box angel-hair pasta

½ cup vegetable or olive oil

½ cup lemon juice

1 tablespoon seasoned salt

½ cup mayonnaise

1 green bell pepper, chopped

1 cup grape tomatoes

1 red onion, chopped

1 cup grated cheddar cheese

½ cup black olives, sliced

Pepperoni, optional

1. Cook pasta according to instructions on package.

2. Mix oil, lemon juice, seasoned salt, and mayonnaise together. Add to drained pasta while it is still warm.

3. When pasta mixture has cooled for at least 30 minutes, stir in pepper, tomatoes, onion, cheese, olives, and pepperoni, if using. Chill.

Pasta à la Carbonara

Hope Comerford,
Clinton Township, MI

Makes 8 servings
Prep. Time: 10 minutes
Cooking/Baking Time: 8 hours
Ideal slow-cooker size: 4- to 6-qt.

1 package thick-cut bacon, sliced into bite-size pieces

1 chicken bouillon cube

2 teaspoons garlic powder

1 teaspoon (or less depending on the level of heat you prefer) crushed red pepper flakes

1 pound rotini pasta

¼ cup of pasta water (the water you cook the pasta in)

2 egg yolks

½ teaspoon pepper

¼ cup grated Parmesan cheese

½ cup flat-leaf parsley, chopped

1. Place cut-up bacon in bottom of slow-cooker crock. Try to separate it as much as you can so pieces are not all completely stuck together. Cover and cook on Low for 7 hours.

2. The last 30 to 45 minutes of cooking, turn slow cooker up to High and add bouillon cube, garlic powder, and crushed red pepper flakes. Stir.

3. Cook pasta according to instructions on package. When pasta is done, reserve ¼ cup of water.

4. In a bowl, mix together egg yolks, pepper, and Parmesan cheese. Next, whisk in ¼ cup pasta water to temper egg yolks.

5. Pour pasta into the slow cooker, pour egg/Parmesan mixture over the top, and toss in parsley. Mix well.

Pasta with Veggies

STOVETOP OVEN

Ricotta Gnocchi with Spinach Sauce

Judy Hershberger,
Millersburg, OH

Makes 4 servings
Prep. Time: 35 minutes
Cooking/Baking Time: 40 minutes

2 tablespoons butter

1 large onion, halved and thinly sliced

1½ cups, plus 1 tablespoon, all-purpose flour, divided

2 cups half-and-half

½ teaspoon ground nutmeg

5 ounces baby spinach, rinsed and dried

15 ounces ricotta cheese

3 large eggs

1 cup grated Parmesan cheese, divided

1 teaspoon salt

½ teaspoon pepper

1. Bring large Dutch oven of salted water to a boil.

2. Meanwhile, in large, ovenproof skillet, melt butter over medium-low heat.

3. Add onion and cook, stirring occasionally, until softened and golden, 10 to 12 minutes.

4. Add 1 tablespoon flour and cook, stirring constantly, 2 minutes.

5. Add half-and-half and simmer, stirring constantly, until slightly thickened, for about 3 minutes.

6. Add nutmeg.

7. Working in batches, stir in spinach and cook over low heat until just wilted, 3 to 5 minutes. Cover and set sauce aside.

8. In a medium bowl, lightly beat together ricotta, eggs, ½ cup Parmesan, the remaining 1½ cups flour, salt, and pepper. Stir until well combined.

9. Using a soup spoon, drop 10 to 12 generous spoonfuls of dough (about half the dough) into the boiling water. Cook for 3 minutes. Gently stir the gnocchi to keep them from clumping together.

10. When the gnocchi rise to the surface, cook for about 3 minutes more.

11. Using a slotted spoon, transfer gnocchi to a towel-lined plate to drain. Repeat process with the remaining dough.

12. Add the cooked gnocchi to the spinach sauce and stir gently to coat.

13. Transfer mixture to a baking dish. Sprinkle with the remaining ½ cup Parmesan.

14. Broil until golden, about 3 minutes.

Super Easy Pasta!

Tortellini with Broccoli

**Susan Kasting,
Jenks, OK**

Makes 4 servings
Prep. Time: 10 minutes
Cooking/Baking Time: 2½–3 hours
Ideal slow-cooker size: 4-qt.

½ cup water

26-ounce jar pasta sauce, divided

1 tablespoon Italian seasoning

9-ounce package frozen spinach and cheese
   tortellini

16-ounce package frozen broccoli florets

1. In a bowl, mix water, pasta sauce, and seasoning together.

2. Pour ⅓ of sauce into bottom of slow cooker. Top with tortellini.

3. Pour ⅓ of sauce over tortellini. Top with broccoli.

4. Pour remaining sauce over broccoli.

5. Cook on High for 2½ to 3 hours, or until broccoli and pasta are tender but not mushy.

STOVETOP

Penne alla Vodka

**Abigail Lawrence,
Marlboro, VT**

Makes 4 servings
Prep. Time: 10 minutes
Cooking/Baking Time: 15 minutes

8 ounces penne pasta

1 tablespoon butter

½ small onion, finely chopped

1 garlic clove, minced

¼ teaspoon crushed red pepper

¼ cup vodka

6-ounce can tomato paste

1 cup heavy cream

1 cup frozen peas

¼ cup grated Parmesan

1. Cook pasta according to instructions on package. Drain and return to pot to keep warm.

2. In saucepan, melt butter. Add onion, garlic, and crushed red pepper. Sauté until onions are soft and garlic is fragrant.

3. Add vodka and simmer for about 30 seconds.

4. Stir in tomato paste and then reduce heat to low and stir in heavy cream.

5. Stir in peas and cook just until peas are tender, then remove from heat.

6. In large bowl, toss together pasta and sauce.

7. Fold in grated Parmesan.

Pasta Vanesa

**Barry Coggin,
Jacksonville, FL**

Makes 6 servings
Prep. Time: 30 minutes
Cooking/Baking Time: 1 hour and 45 minutes

2 medium onions, chopped

1 yellow bell pepper, chopped

1 orange bell pepper, chopped

3 garlic cloves, thinly sliced

10.75-ounce can tomato purée

3 (8-ounce) cans tomato sauce

6-ounce can tomato paste

1 package (5 links) sweet Italian sausage, chopped

3 links hot Italian sausage, chopped

Salt, to taste

Pepper, to taste

1½ teaspoons Italian seasoning

2 tablespoons honey

1 cup water

16-ounce package spaghetti

1 cup whipping cream

¼ cup fresh chopped parsley

1. In large nonstick skillet, sauté onions, bell peppers, and garlic until just tender.

2. Add tomato purée, sauce, and paste. Blend well. Simmer covered for 1 hour.

3. Meanwhile, in a separate skillet, brown sausages. Add to tomato mixture.

4. Season with salt, pepper, and Italian seasoning. Then stir in honey and water.

5. Simmer covered for 30 minutes. Meanwhile, cook spaghetti according to instructions on package. Drain.

6. Just before serving, add whipping cream to tomato mixture. Cook until heated through, but do not boil.

7. Serve tomato sauce over cooked spaghetti. Sprinkle with fresh parsley.

Lemon Ricotta Pasta with Peas

**Abigail Lawrence,
Marlboro, VT**

Makes 4 servings
Prep. Time: 10 minutes
Cooking/Baking Time: 15 minutes

8 ounces penne

1 cup frozen peas

1½ cups (12 ounces) whole milk ricotta

¾ cups grated Parmesan cheese

Juice and zest of 1 lemon

¾ teaspoon salt

¼ teaspoon black pepper

1. Cook pasta according to instructions on package. About 2 minutes before pasta is done, add frozen peas. Reserve 2 cups pasta water before draining.

2. While pasta is cooking, combine ricotta, Parmesan, lemon juice, 2 teaspoons lemon zest, salt, and pepper.

3. In a large bowl, add ricotta mixture to pasta along with ½ cup of reserved pasta water. Toss together. Add more of the reserved pasta water as needed to make a smooth sauce.

Minestra Di Ceci

Jeanette Oberholtzer
Manheim, PA

Makes 8 servings
Soaking Time: 8 hours
Prep. Time: 20 minutes
Cooking/Baking Time: 5½–6 hours
Ideal slow-cooker size: 4-qt.

1 pound dry chickpeas

1 sprig fresh rosemary

10 leaves fresh sage

1 tablespoon salt

1–2 large garlic cloves, minced

1 teaspoon olive oil

1 cup small dry pasta, your choice of shape

1. Wash chickpeas. Place in slow cooker. Soak for 8 hours in full pot of water, along with rosemary, sage, and salt.

2. Drain water. Remove herbs.

3. Refill slow cooker with water to 1 inch above peas.

4. Cover. Cook on Low for 5 hours.

5. Sauté garlic in olive oil in skillet until clear.

6. Purée ½ of chickpeas, along with several cups of broth from cooker, in blender. Return purée to slow cooker. Add garlic and oil.

7. Boil pasta in saucepan until al dente. Drain. Add to beans.

8. Cover. Cook on High for 30 to 60 minutes, or until pasta is tender and heated through, but not mushy.

Fettuccine with Butter-Herb Sauce

**Stacy Stoltzfus,
Grantham, PA**

Makes 3–4 servings
Prep. Time: 5 minutes
Cooking/Baking Time: 8–10 minutes

⅓ pound fettuccine

4 tablespoons butter, melted

1 tablespoon, or more, fresh basil

¾ teaspoon fresh chopped thyme

¼ cup fresh parsley

1 tablespoon chives, optional

1. Cook fettuccine according to instructions on package.

2. Meanwhile blend remaining ingredients in a small pitcher.

3. Drain noodles very well when done and transfer to a serving bowl.

4. Pour melted butter with herbs over noodles. Toss and serve immediately.

TIP

For best flavor, use fresh herbs. Feel free to alter the amounts to your own taste. You may also substitute extra- virgin olive oil for the butter.

Penne with Herb, Cheese, and Spinach

**Barbara A. Nolan,
Pleasant Valley, NY**

Makes 4 servings
Prep. Time: 10 minutes
Cooking/Baking Time: 25–30 minutes

¾ pound penne pasta

2 tablespoons olive oil

2 tablespoons minced garlic

10 ounces fresh baby spinach, washed

5- to 6-ounce container garlic/herb cheese spread

¾ cup pasta cooking water

Salt, to taste, optional

Pepper, to taste, optional

1. Cook pasta according to instructions on package. Set aside ½ cup cooking water. Drain the rest of the water off, and keep pasta warm.

2. In large stockpot, heat olive oil.

3. Cook minced garlic until soft, 5 to 6 minutes. Do not brown.

4. Add spinach and cook until wilted, about 3 to 4 minutes.

5. Coarsely chop spinach.

6. Add cheese spread and water from pasta to spinach in pan. Cook over medium-low heat, stirring to melt cheese.

7. Add cooked pasta to spinach/cheese mixture.

8. Season with salt and pepper, if using.

9. Toss gently. Serve immediately.

Pasta Primavera

**Marcia S. Myer,
Manheim, PA**

Makes 6 servings
Prep. Time: 20–30 minutes
Cooking/Baking Time: 25 minutes

3 cups broccoli florets, cut into bite-size pieces

½ pound fresh mushrooms, quartered

2 small zucchini, sliced into ¼-inch-thick rounds

1 tablespoon olive oil

1–3 garlic cloves, minced, according to your taste
    preference

1 pint cherry tomatoes, halved

8-ounce package whole-grain fettuccine

Pepper, to taste

3 tablespoons grated reduced-fat Parmesan
    cheese

Sauce:

¾ cup skim milk

1 tablespoon olive oil

⅔ cup part-skim ricotta cheese

¼ cup grated reduced-fat Parmesan cheese

2 tablespoons chopped fresh basil or 1 tablespoon
    dried basil

2 teaspoons dry sherry

1. In large microwave-safe bowl, layer broccoli, mushrooms, and zucchini. Cover bowl and microwave on High for 2 minutes.

2. Stir. Cover and cook another 2 minutes on High, or until tender-crisp.

3. In nonstick skillet, heat olive oil. Add garlic and sauté for 1 minute. Add tomatoes and sauté for 2 minutes, or until tomatoes are slightly cooked but not wilted.

4. Cook fettuccine as directed with no salt. Drain. Keep warm.

5. Prepare sauce by combining milk, oil, ricotta cheese, Parmesan cheese, basil, and sherry in a blender.

6. Process until smooth. Heat sauce until warm, on stove or in microwave.

7. In large serving bowl, toss drained pasta, vegetables, and sauce.

8. Garnish with black pepper and Parmesan cheese.

STOVETOP

Pasta with Fresh Tomatoes and Basil

**Naomi Cunningham,
Arlington, KS**

Makes 2 servings
Prep. Time: 5 minutes
Standing Time: 2–3 hours
Cooking/Baking Time: 15 minutes

2 large fresh tomatoes, chopped

2 tablespoons snipped fresh basil

1 garlic clove, minced

¼ teaspoon pepper

4 ounces dry farfalle or other, pasta, cooked and drained additional fresh basil, optional

1. In mixing bowl, combine tomatoes, basil, garlic, and pepper.

2. Set aside at room temperature for several hours.

3. Serve over hot cooked pasta.

4. Garnish with additional basil, if using.

Tomato-y Penne Pasta

Joy Sutter,
Perkasie, PA

Makes 8 servings
Serving size is 1¼ cups
Prep Time: 15 minutes
Cooking/Baking Time: 25 minutes

1 tablespoon butter

1 tablespoon olive oil

1 small onion, chopped

28-ounce can Italian plum tomatoes, drained, seeded, and chopped

1 cup fat-free half-and-half

¼ cup vodka

¼ teaspoon dried crushed red pepper flakes

Salt, to taste

Pepper, to taste

1 pound penne pasta

¼ cup, or more, freshly grated Parmesan cheese

2 tablespoons, or more, minced fresh chives

1. In large heavy saucepan, melt butter with oil over medium heat.

2. Add onion and sauté until translucent. Add tomatoes and cook uncovered until almost no liquid remains.

3. Stir in half-and-half, vodka, and red pepper flakes, and boil until the mixture reaches a sauce consistency, about 2 minutes. Add salt and pepper to taste.

4. Meanwhile, cook pasta according to instructions on package. Drain.

5. Pour hot sauce over cooked pasta.

6. Toss and sprinkle with Parmesan cheese and chives.

Broccoli Noodle Supreme

**Virginia Blish,
Akron, NY**

Makes 6 servings
Prep Time: 10 minutes
Cooking/Baking Time: 15 minutes

3 cups egg noodles

2 cups broccoli florets

10.75-ounce can condensed cream of chicken-
and-broccoli or cream of chicken, soup

½ cup sour cream

⅓ cup grated Parmesan cheese

⅛ teaspoon pepper, optional

1. In saucepan, cook noodles according to instructions on package. Add broccoli during the noodles' last 5 minutes of cooking.

2. Drain and set aside. Keep warm.

3. In same saucepan, combine soup, sour cream, Parmesan cheese, and pepper, if using. Cook and stir until heated through.

4. Remove from heat and stir in noodles and broccoli mixture. Mix thoroughly and serve.

Asparagus Fettuccine

**Melva Baumer,
Mifflintown, PA**

Makes 2 servings
Prep. Time: 15 minutes
Cooking/Baking Time: 15–20 minutes

4 ounces fettuccine

½ pound fresh asparagus, cut in 1-inch pieces

¼ cup chopped onions

1 garlic clove, minced

1 tablespoon butter

2 ounces cream cheese, cubed

¼ cup fat-free milk

¼ cup shredded Parmesan cheese

1½ teaspoons lemon juice

¼ teaspoon salt

⅛ teaspoon pepper

1. Cook fettuccine according to instructions on package. Drain.

2. In large skillet, sauté asparagus, onions, and garlic in butter until tender.

3. Add cream cheese, milk, Parmesan cheese, lemon juice, salt, and pepper.

4. Cook and stir over medium heat for 5 minutes or until cheese is melted and sauce is blended.

5. Toss fettuccine with asparagus mixture.

Daddy's Pasta Fasool

**Maria Shevlin,
Sicklerville, NJ**

Makes 8 servings
Prep. Time: 15 minutes
Cooking/Baking Time: 6 minutes
Setting: Sauté and Manual
Pressure: High
Release: Manual

1 cup tomato sauce

1 cup diced onion

½ cup diced carrots

½ cup diced celery

1 tablespoon chopped fresh celery leaves

14.5-ounce can petite diced tomatoes

1 cup precooked ground turkey

3–4 garlic cloves, minced

1 bay leaf

½ teaspoon onion powder

½ teaspoon garlic powder

¼ teaspoon basil

¼ teaspoon oregano

½ teaspoon parsley flakes

½ teaspoon salt

¼ teaspoon black pepper

15.5-ounce can cannelini beans, drained and
  rinsed (I use Goya brand)

1 cup elbows or similar small pasta of your choice

4 cups chicken bone broth

1. In inner pot of the Instant Pot, combine sauce, vegetables, tomatoes, meat, and seasonings, and stir.

2. Set to Sauté for 5 minutes, stirring occasionally.

3. After 5 minutes, add beans, pasta, and bone broth, in that order.

4. Lock lid, set vent to sealing, then set on Manual at high pressure for 6 minutes.

5. Release pressure manually when cooking time is over.

SERVING SUGGESTION

Serve with a buttered roll and top with fresh grated Parmesan cheese.

STOVETOP

Parmesan Noodles

**Jan Mast,
Lancaster, PA**

Makes 4-6 servings
Prep. Time: 7 minutes
Cooking/Baking Time: 10 minutes

8 ounces fettuccine

¾ stick (6 tablespoons) butter, melted

1 cup Parmesan cheese

¼ teaspoon garlic salt

½ cup light cream

1 teaspoon parsley, optional

1. Cook noodles according to instructions on package. Drain. Return noodles to stockpot.

2. Stir in remaining ingredients, except parsley. Toss to mix.

3. Just before serving, garnish with parsley, if using.

Sesame Noodles

**Sheila Ann Plock,
Boalsburg, PA**

Makes 10–12 servings
Prep. Time: 15 minutes
Chilling Time: 8 hours or overnight
Cooking/Baking Time: 11 minutes

¼ cup soy sauce

3 tablespoons sesame oil, divided

2 tablespoons red wine vinegar

2 tablespoons olive oil

1½ tablespoons sugar

1 tablespoon prepared chili sauce with garlic

12-ounce box linguine noodles

4 scallions

1 red bell pepper, cut into thin match-stick strips

1. One day before serving noodles, combine 2 tablespoons soy sauce, sesame oil, vinegar, olive oil, sugar, and chili sauce in food processor or blender. Blend until well combined.

2. Cover. Chill in refrigerator for 8 hours or overnight to allow flavors to blend.

3. Cook noodles according to instructions on package. Rinse, drain, and cool.

4. In large bowl, toss cooked noodles with 1 tablespoon sesame oil.

5. Stir in scallions and bell pepper strips.

6. Toss with enough dressing to coat.

7. Serve chilled or at room temperature.

Greek Pasta Salad

Edie Moran,
West Babylon, NY
Judi Manos,
West Islip, NY

Makes 8 servings
Prep. Time: 15 minutes
Cooking/Baking Time: 15 minutes

1 cup farfalle (bow-tie) pasta

4 medium plum tomatoes, chopped

15-ounce can chickpeas, rinsed and drained

1 medium onion, chopped

6-ounce can pitted black olives, drained

4-ounce package feta cheese, crumbled

1 garlic clove, minced

½ cup olive oil

¼ cup lemon juice

1 teaspoon salt

½ teaspoon pepper

1. Cook pasta according to instructions on package. Drain.

2. In large bowl, combine pasta, tomatoes, chickpeas, onion, olives, feta cheese, and garlic.

3. In small bowl, whisk together oil, lemon juice, salt, and pepper. Pour over salad and toss to coat.

4. Cover and chill in refrigerator. Stir before serving.

VARIATION

Add some baby spinach leaves to the hot pasta right after draining it.

Pasta with Seafood

STOVETOP

Shrimp with Sun-Dried Tomatoes

Josie Healy,
Middle Village, NY

Makes 3-4 servings
Prep. Time: 10 minutes
Cooking/Baking Time: 10 minutes

8 ounces linguine

2 tablespoons olive oil

1 pound cleaned and peeled shrimp

2 garlic cloves, minced

¼ cup white wine

6-8 sun-dried tomatoes, chopped (use dry tomatoes, not in oil)

1. Cook linguine according to instructions on package. Drain and keep warm.

2. While pasta is cooking, place olive oil in large skillet and heat. Carefully add shrimp and garlic, being careful not to splatter yourself with the hot oil.

3. Sauté, stirring constantly, until shrimp is slightly pink and garlic is softened.

4. Stir in wine and sun-dried tomatoes. Cook another 1 to 2 minutes over low heat.

5. If you'd like more liquid, add ¼ cup water, more wine, or chicken stock.

6. Serve shrimp and sauce over pasta.

Quick Shrimp Pasta

**Sandra Chang,
Derwood, MD**

Makes 4–6 servings
Prep. Time: 30 minutes
Cooking/Baking Time: 20 minutes

1 pound spaghetti

1 tablespoon vegetable oil

1 pound raw shrimp, peeled and deveined

Kosher salt

Ground black pepper

1 medium zucchini, unpeeled and cut into ½-inch
  pieces

3 garlic cloves, minced

½ cup extra-virgin olive oil

⅓ cup fresh flat-leaf parsley

½ teaspoon cracked black pepper

1 cup grated Parmesan cheese, divided

1. Cook spaghetti according to instructions on package. When finished cooking, drain, return to cooking pot, and keep warm.

2. Meanwhile, in a large skillet, heat vegetable oil over high heat until smoking hot.

3. Place shrimp in pan and sear for 1 to 2 minutes per side, or until just cooked through. Stir in a dash of kosher salt and a dash of pepper. Remove seasoned shrimp to a large serving bowl and keep warm.

4. Sauté zucchini pieces and minced garlic briefly in skillet until crisp-tender.

5. Add zucchini and garlic to shrimp.

6. Mix in olive oil, garlic, parsley, pepper, and ½ cup Parmesan cheese.

7. Add cooked pasta and remaining cheese. Toss well and serve.

VARIATION

Substitute 1½ lb. scallops for the shrimp, or mix the two.

Slow-Cooker Shrimp Marinara

Judy Miles,
Centreville, MD

Makes 6 servings
Prep. Time: 10–15 minutes
Cooking/Baking Time: 3¼–4¼ hours
Ideal slow-cooker size: 3½-qt.

16-ounce can low-sodium chopped tomatoes

2 tablespoons minced fresh parsley

1 garlic clove, minced

½ teaspoon dried basil

½ teaspoon salt

¼ teaspoon black pepper

1 teaspoon dried oregano

6-ounce can tomato paste

½ teaspoon seasoned salt

1 pound shrimp, cooked and shelled

3 cups cooked spaghetti (about 6 ounces dry)

Grated Parmesan cheese, for garnish

1. Combine tomatoes, parsley, garlic, basil, salt, pepper, oregano, tomato paste, and seasoned salt in slow cooker.

2. Cover. Cook on Low for 3 to 4 hours.

3. Stir shrimp into sauce.

4. Cover. Cook on High for 10 to 15 minutes.

5. Serve over cooked spaghetti. Top with Parmesan cheese.

Simple Shrimp Scampi

Anne Jones,
Ballston Lake, NY

Makes 4 servings
Prep Time: 5 minutes
Cooking/Baking Time: 35 minutes

8 ounces rotini or pasta of your choice

2 tablespoons olive oil

2 garlic cloves, crushed

1 tablespoon lemon juice

1 tablespoon dried parsley

1 pound shrimp, shelled and deveined

2 tablespoons freshly grated Parmesan cheese, divided

1. Cook pasta according to instructions on package. Drain.

2. While pasta is cooking, in a large skillet or wok, heat olive oil over low heat.

3. Add garlic, lemon juice, and parsley. Cook until garlic is tender.

4. Add shrimp and 1 tablespoon Parmesan cheese. Cook over low heat until shrimp becomes opaque, stirring frequently, about 3 minutes.

5. Serve shrimp and sauce over pasta. Sprinkle with 1 tablespoon Parmesan cheese.

Shrimp and Mushroom Linguine

**Cyndie Marrara,
Port Matilda, PA**

Makes 4 servings
Prep Time: 10 minutes
Cooking/Baking Time: 30 minutes

8 ounces linguine

2 cups fresh sliced mushrooms

1 stick (½ cup) butter

¼ cup flour

⅛ teaspoon pepper

3 cups milk

2 cups peeled and cooked shrimp

¼ cup Parmesan cheese, plus more for serving

1. Cook linguine according to instructions on package. Drain and keep warm.

2. While pasta is cooking, sauté mushrooms in butter in a large skillet. Blend in flour and pepper.

3. Add milk, and stir constantly until thickened.

4. Add shrimp and Parmesan cheese. Heat thoroughly.

5. Combine shrimp sauce with linguine. Toss lightly and sprinkle with additional Parmesan cheese.

STOVETOP

Spaghetti with Clam Sauce

**Susan Kasting,
Jenks, OK**

Makes 4 servings
Prep. Time: 5 minutes
Cooking/Baking Time: 20 minutes

16-ounce package spaghetti

2 sticks (1 cup) butter

3 garlic cloves, minced

2 (6-ounce) cans chopped clams, with juice

½ cup chopped fresh parsley

1. Cook spaghetti al dente according to instructions on package.

2. In saucepan, melt butter. Stir in garlic and sauté briefly.

3. Add clams and parsley. Heat just until hot throughout.

4. Drain spaghetti and return to cooking pot. Pour sauce over noodles and mix through.

5. Let stand for a few minutes so the pasta can absorb some of the sauce.

VARIATION

Replace 1 stick of butter with ½ cup dry white wine.

STOVETOP

Pasta with White Clam Sauce

Anne Jones,
Ballston Lake, NY

Makes 8 servings
Prep Time: 20 minutes
Cooking/Baking Time: 20 minutes

16-ounce package linguine

2 tablespoons canola oil

4 garlic cloves, crushed

½ cup diced onions

2 tablespoons flour

2 (6-ounce) cans chopped clams

1 cup milk

¾ teaspoon salt

¼–½ teaspoon pepper

1 tablespoon parsley

Shredded Parmesan cheese, optional

1. Cook pasta according to instructions on package. Drain and keep warm.

2. While pasta is cooking, in a medium saucepan, heat oil. Sauté garlic and onions until tender.

3. Add flour and stir until smooth.

4. Drain clams, reserving liquid.

5. Stir milk and reserved clam juice into flour mixture. Continue heating over medium heat, stirring constantly until thickened.

6. Add salt, pepper, parsley, and clams. Warm through.

7. Place linguine in large serving bowl. Stir clam sauce into it. Sprinkle with shredded Parmesan cheese, if using.

Company Seafood Pasta

**Jennifer Yoder Sommers,
Harrisonburg, VA**

Makes 8 servings
Prep. Time: 35 minutes
Cooking/Baking Time: 1–2 hours
Ideal slow-cooker size: 4-qt.

2 cups sour cream

1¼ cups shredded Monterey Jack cheese

1 tablespoon butter, melted

½ pound fresh crabmeat

⅛ teaspoon pepper

½ pound bay scallops, lightly cooked

1 pound medium shrimp, cooked and peeled

16 ounces linguine

Fresh parsley, for garnish

1. Combine sour cream, cheese, and butter in slow cooker.

2. Stir in remaining ingredients, except linguine and parsley.

3. Cover. Cook on Low for 1 to 2 hours.

4. Cook linguine according to instructions on package. Drain.

5. Serve seafood sauce over linguine. Garnish with fresh parsley.

Baked Pasta Dishes

STOVETOP OVEN

Florentine Roll-Ups

**Elaine Rineer,
Lancaster, PA**

Makes 12 servings
Prep. Time: 35–45 minutes
Baking Time: 45 minutes

16-ounce package lasagna noodles

4 cups (2 pounds) ricotta or cottage cheese

2 cups (8 ounces) grated cheddar cheese

1 cup cleaned, well drained, and chopped fresh
   spinach

½ cup chopped scallions

1 egg, beaten

¼ teaspoon black pepper

¼ teaspoon salt

3 cups spaghetti sauce, your favorite flavor or
   homemade (page 3), divided

Parmesan cheese

1. Cook pasta according to instructions on package. Drain. Lay flat on waxed paper to cool.

2. In large mixing bowl, stir together ricotta, cheddar cheese, spinach, scallions, egg, pepper, and salt.

3. Spread ⅓ cup mixture on each lasagna noodle. Roll up. Secure with toothpick if needed to keep from unrolling.

4. Spread ⅔ cup spaghetti sauce on bottom of well-greased 9×13-inch baking pan.

5. Place rolls seam-side down in pan.

6. Top with remaining sauce. Sprinkle with Parmesan cheese.

7. Cover. Bake at 350°F for 45 minutes.

Stuffed Pasta Shells

Jean M. Butzer, Batavia, NY
Lori Lehman, Ephrata, PA
Rhoda Atzeff, Lancaster, PA

Makes 12–14 servings
Prep. Time: 30–45 minutes
Cooking/Baking Time: 30–45 minutes

1 pound shredded mozzarella cheese

15-ounce container ricotta cheese

10-ounce package frozen chopped spinach, thawed and squeezed dry

12-ounce package jumbo pasta shells, cooked and drained

28-ounce jar spaghetti sauce

1. In a large mixing bowl, combine cheeses and spinach.

2. Stuff a rounded tablespoonful into each shell.

3. Arrange filled shells in a greased 9×13-inch baking dish.

4. Pour spaghetti sauce over the shells.

5. Cover and bake at 350°F for 30 to 45 minutes, or until heated through.

OVEN

Mostaccioli

**Sally Holzem,
Schofield, WI**

Makes 8 servings
Prep. Time: 45 minutes
Baking Time: 30–45 minutes

½ pound bulk Italian sausage

½ cup chopped onion

16-ounce can tomato paste

½ cup water

½ teaspoon oregano

¼ teaspoon pepper

4-ounce can sliced
  mushrooms, drained

14.5-ounce can diced
  tomatoes

¾ cup tomato juice

8-ounce package mostaccioli
  noodles, divided

1½ cups cottage cheese

½ teaspoon marjoram

12 ounces shredded
  mozzarella cheese, divided

¼ cup grated Parmesan
  cheese

1. In saucepan, brown sausage and onion, stirring often to break up clumps. When pink no longer remains, drain off drippings.

2. Stir in tomato paste, water, oregano, pepper, mushrooms, tomatoes and their juices, and tomato juice.

3. Cover. Simmer for 30 minutes over medium heat.

4. Meanwhile, prepare noodles according to instructions on package. Drain well.

5. In mixing bowl, combine cottage cheese and marjoram.

6. In greased 7x13-inch baking pan, layer in half of noodles.

7. Top with half of meat sauce.

8. Sprinkle with half of mozzarella.

9. Spoon cottage cheese mixture over top and spread as well as you can.

10. Layer on remaining noodles.

11. Top with remaining meat sauce.

12. Sprinkle with remaining mozzarella cheese.

13. Sprinkle with Parmesan cheese.

14. Bake at 350°F for 30 to 45 minutes, or until bubbly, heated through, and lightly browned.

Super-Creamy Macaroni and Cheese

Jean Butzer,
Batavia, NY
Arlene Leaman Kliewer,
Lakewood, CO
Esther Burkholder,
Millerstown, PA
Hazel Lightcap Propst,
Oxford, PA
Karla Baer,
North Lima, OH

Makes 8–10 servings
Prep. Time: 5–10 minutes
Baking Time: 1 hour 20 minutes

Butter for greasing casserole

1 pound elbow macaroni

4 cups shredded cheddar cheese or ½ pound
  cubed Velveeta cheese

2 (10.75-ounce) cans cheddar cheese, soup or
  cream of celery, soup

3½ cups milk

1½ cups chopped cooked ham, optional

1 teaspoon salt, optional

¼ teaspoon pepper, optional

1. Combine all ingredients in a buttered 3-quart casserole or baking dish.

2. Cover and bake at 350°F for 1 hour.

3. Stir up from bottom.

4. Bake uncovered an additional 20 minutes.

STOVETOP OVEN

Zesty Macaroni and Cheese

**Rosemarie Fitzgerald,
Gibsonia, PA**

Makes 4 servings
Prep. Time: 15 minutes
Cooking/Baking Time: 40 minutes

4-ounce package whole wheat elbow macaroni

1¼ cups hot milk

½ pound cheddar cheese, shredded

6 tablespoons dry bread crumbs or 3/4 cup fresh
   crumbs

2 tablespoons chopped fresh parsley

1 medium onion, chopped

1 green bell pepper, finely chopped

3–4 scallions, chopped, or more to taste

1 teaspoon salt, optional

2 eggs, beaten

Paprika

1. Cook macaroni until al dente. Drain and set aside.

2. In large bowl, pour hot milk over cheese and crumbs.

3. Add parsley, onion, pepper, scallions, and salt, if using.

4. Stir in eggs and cooked macaroni.

5. Pour into lightly greased 3-quart casserole dish. Sprinkle with paprika.

6. Bake at 350°F for 30 minutes, or until the top of the casserole is firm and golden brown.

Veggie Macaroni and Cheese

**Dorothy Lingerfelt,
Stonyford, CA**

Makes 12 servings
Prep. Time: 30 minutes
Cooking/Baking Time: 30 minutes

1½ cups elbow macaroni

3 cups chopped broccoli

2 cups chopped
    cauliflower

3 carrots, thinly sliced

2 celery ribs, sliced

1 medium onion, diced

1 tablespoon butter

¼ cup all-purpose flour

1 cup milk

3 cups shredded cheddar
    cheese

1 tablespoon Dijon mustard

¼ teaspoon pepper

¼ teaspoon paprika

1. In large pot of salted boiling water, cook macaroni for 1 to 2 minutes.

2. Add broccoli, cauliflower, carrots, and celery and cook 5 more minutes.

3. Drain, but reserve 1 cup cooking water.

4. Pour vegetables and macaroni into lightly greased 9×13-inch baking pan. Set aside.

5. Meanwhile, in a saucepan, sauté onions in butter until tender.

6. Sprinkle with flour and stir until blended.

7. Over low heat, gradually stir in milk and reserved 1 cup cooking water.

8. Bring to boil over medium heat, stirring. Cook and stir for 2 minutes, or until thickened.

9. Turn off heat. Stir in cheese, mustard, and pepper.

10. Pour sauce over macaroni mixture in pan. Stir to coat. Spread evenly in pan.

11. Sprinkle with paprika.

12. Bake uncovered at 350°F for 15 to 20 minutes or until heated through.

Slow Cooker Macaroni and Cheese

**Lisa F. Good,
Harrisonburg, VA**

Makes 6 servings
Prep. Time: 10 minutes
Cooking/Baking Time: 3–4 hours
Ideal slow-cooker size: 4-qt.

1½ cups dry macaroni

1½ tablespoons butter

6 ounces Velveeta cheese, sliced

2 cups milk

1 cup half-and-half

1. Combine macaroni and butter.

2. Layer cheese over top.

3. Pour in milk and half-and-half.

4. Cover. Cook on High for 3 to 4 hours, or until macaroni is soft.

Household-Size Ziti Bake

Joy Reiff,
Mount Joy, PA

Makes 6–8 servings
Prep. Time: 30 minutes
Baking Time: 45–60 minutes

16-ounce package ziti or rigatoni

1¼ pound ground beef

1 pound ricotta or cottage cheese

½ cup grated Parmesan cheese

3 tablespoons chopped fresh parsley

1 egg, beaten

½ teaspoon salt

¼–½ teaspoon pepper, according to your taste preference

6 cups spaghetti sauce (store-bought or homemade, page 3)

½ pound mozzarella, shredded

1. Prepare ziti according to instructions on package. Drain and set aside.

2. Brown ground beef. Stir frequently to break up clumps. Cook until pink no longer remains. Drain off drippings.

3. Stir in ricotta cheese, Parmesan cheese, parsley, egg, salt, and pepper.

4. Add spaghetti sauce. Stir until well mixed.

5. Add ziti. Toss gently to coat well.

6. Spoon into greased 9x13-inch baking pan.

7. Pour remaining spaghetti sauce over ziti mixture. Sprinkle with mozzarella.

8. Bake at 350°F for 45 to 60 minutes, or until bubbly and heated through.

Baked Pasta with Chicken Sausage

**Kim Rapp,
Longmont, CO**

Makes 8 servings
Prep. Time: 40 minutes
Baking Time: 20–30 minutes

1 pound rigatoni

10-ounce package fresh baby spinach

1 tablespoon olive oil

1 medium red onion, chopped

4 garlic cloves, minced

¼ cup vodka, optional

28-ounce can whole tomatoes with juice, lightly crushed with hands or 2 pounds whole tomatoes, peeled

1½ teaspoons fresh chopped oregano

½ cup heavy cream

12-ounce smoked chicken sausage, halved lengthwise then cut into ¼-inch-thick slices

6 ounces fontina cheese: 4 ounces cubed; 2 ounces shredded

Salt

Pepper

¼ cup grated Parmesan cheese

1. Cook rigatoni according to instructions on package.

2. Stir in baby spinach. Continue cooking for 3 minutes. Drain pasta and spinach well. Return to cooking pot and keep warm.

3. In large skillet over medium heat, heat oil. Add onion. Cook about 3 minutes.

4. Stir in garlic. Remove from heat.

5. Add vodka, if using. Return to fairly high heat and cook until liquid is almost evaporated, about 1 minute.

6. Stir in tomatoes and oregano. Cook for 10 to 15 minutes.

7. Add cream and warm, cooking gently about 5 minutes.

8. Add sausage and cubed fontina to pot. Toss to coat.

9. Season with several grinds of salt and pepper.

10. Divide evenly between two greased 1½-quart baking dishes, or spoon into 1 greased 9×13-inch baking dish.

11. Top with grated fontina and Parmesan cheeses.

12. Bake at 400°F until browned, about 20 to 30 minutes.

TIP

Add ¼ cup water or broth if mixture seems dry before baking.

Instant Pot Shells & Cheese with Kale

Cynthia Hockman-Chupp,
Canby, OR

Makes 6–8 servings
Prep. Time: 5 minutes
Cooking/Baking Time: 20 minutes
Setting: Manual
Pressure: High
Release: Manual

1 pound uncooked medium pasta shells

2 tablespoons butter

½ teaspoon curry powder

½ teaspoon dry mustard powder

1 teaspoon hot pepper sauce

2 teaspoons salt

4 cups water

12-ounce can evaporated milk

16 ounces shredded cheddar cheese

6 ounces shredded Parmesan cheese

1 tablespoon yellow mustard

1–2 cups frozen/thawed, chopped kale

1. In the inner pot of Instant Pot, combine pasta shells, butter, curry power, dry mustard powder, hot pepper sauce, salt, and water.

2. Cook on Manual at high pressure for 4 minutes. Quick release the pressure when cooking time ends.

3. Leave pot in Keep Warm mode while you stir in evaporated milk. Then, stir in the cheeses gradually, melting each handful as you go.

4. Add yellow mustard and chopped kale and mix. Once kale is warmed through, the dish is ready to serve.

STOVETOP **OVEN**

Spinach Ravioli Bake

**Susan Segraves,
Lansdale, PA**

Makes 6 servings
Prep. Time: 15 minutes
Cooking/Baking Time: 50 minutes
Standing Time: 10 minutes

6-ounce bag fresh baby spinach

12-ounce package refrigerated cooked turkey
meatballs

28-ounce jar spaghetti sauce (or 3½ cups
homemade, page 3)

1½ cups water

2 (9-ounce) packages refrigerated 4-cheese ravioli,
divided

8-ounce bag shredded mozzarella cheese, divided

1. Heat oven to 375°F. Rinse spinach and shake off excess water. In large skillet over medium heat, heat spinach for 5 minutes, or until wilted.

2. Coarsely chop meatballs and place in large bowl. Add spinach, spaghetti sauce, and 1½ cups water. Stir to combine.

3. Spoon about 2 cups meatball mixture into bottom of lightly greased 2½-quart casserole.

4. Arrange 1 package ravioli over mixture. Sprinkle with ½ cup cheese.

5. Repeat layering using remaining ravioli, meatball mixture, and cheese.

6. Cover with foil. Bake at 375°F for 35 minutes.

7. Uncover and bake 5 minutes longer, or until cheese melts.

8. Let stand 10 minutes before serving.

STOVETOP   OVEN

Creamy Beef and Pasta Casserole

Virginia Graybill,
Hershey, PA

Makes 6 servings, 4-inch square per serving
Prep. Time: 25 minutes
Baking Time: 30 minutes

1 pound 90% lean ground beef

8-ounce package elbow macaroni

8-ounce package cream cheese, softened

10.75 -ounce can cream of mushroom soup

1 cup milk

½ cup no-salt ketchup

1. In nonstick skillet, cook ground beef until no longer pink, stirring frequently to break up clumps. Drain off any drippings.

2. Cook macaroni until al dente according to instructions on package. Drain.

3. In large mixing bowl, combine pasta and beef.

4. In another mixing bowl, blend together cream cheese, soup, milk, and ketchup.

5. Stir sauce into pasta and beef.

6. Pour into greased 9x13-inch baking pan.

7. Bake at 350°F for 30 minutes, or until bubbly and heated through.

Sausage Ziti Bake

Margaret Morris
Middle Village, NY

Makes 8 servings
Prep Time: 15 minutes
Baking Time: 45 minutes

1 pound lean turkey Italian sausage

16-ounce package ziti

2 cups sliced fresh mushrooms

1 large onion, chopped

26-ounce jar tomato and basil pasta sauce (or homemade, page 3)

Salt, to taste

Pepper, to taste

4 ounces mozzarella cheese, shredded

1. In large stockpot, brown sausage.

2. Meanwhile, cook ziti according to the instructions on package. Drain.

3. After sausage is browned, remove it to a bowl and drain off all drippings. Add mushrooms and onion to stockpot. Cook gently until tender.

4. Stir in sauce, sausage, cooked and drained ziti, salt, and pepper. Spoon into a greased 9x13-inch baking dish. Cover.

5. Bake at 350°F for 30 to 40 minutes, or until heated the whole way through.

6. Sprinkle with cheese. Bake uncovered an additional 5 minutes.

Pasta Pizza Pronto

**Shari Jensen,
Fountain, CO**

Makes 6 servings
Prep. Time: 20 minutes
Baking Time: 37–40 minutes

Crust:

2 cups elbow macaroni

3 eggs

⅓ cup finely chopped onions

1 cup shredded cheddar cheese

Topping:

1½ cups prepared pizza or pasta sauce

3-ounce package sliced pepperoni

2.25-ounce can sliced olives, drained

1 cup toppings: mix or match sliced mushrooms, diced cooked ham or chicken, diced bell peppers

1½ cups shredded mozzarella cheese

TIPS

1. Don't overload with toppings. Stay within the 1-cup suggestion.
2. Using the lower shelf of oven will crisp the crust. If not available in your oven, the middle shelf is okay.
3. Keep pasta pieces touching each other; no gaps.

1. In saucepan, cook macaroni according to instructions on package. Drain well.

2. In large bowl, beat eggs. Stir in onions, cheddar cheese, and cooked macaroni.

3. Spread pasta mixture evenly on generously greased 14- to 16-inch pizza pan.

4. Bake at 375°F for 25 minutes on lower oven rack. Remove from oven.

5. Top with your favorite pizza or pasta sauce. Spread to within ½ inch of edge, using the back of a spoon.

6. Top evenly with pepperoni, olives, and 1 cup of the other toppings.

7. Finish by sprinkling with mozzarella cheese.

8. Return to oven and bake for 12 to 15 minutes longer, until cheese is bubbly.

9. Remove from oven and slice with pizza cutter into 6 to 8 slices. Serve warm.

Slow-Cooker Lasagna

**Rachel Yoder,
Middlebury, IN**

Makes 6–8 servings
Prep. Time: 30–45 minutes
Cooking/Baking Time: 4 hours
Ideal slow-cooker size: 6-qt.

Nonstick cooking spray

1 pound extra-lean ground beef

29-ounce can tomato sauce

8-ounce package lasagna noodles, divided

4 cups shredded low-fat mozzarella cheese

1½ cups low-fat cottage cheese

1. Spray interior of the cooker with nonstick spray.

2. In large nonstick skillet, brown ground beef. Drain off drippings.

3. Stir in tomato sauce. Mix well.

4. Spread ¼ of meat sauce on the bottom of the slow cooker.

5. Arrange ⅓ of noodles over sauce. If you wish, break them up so they fit better.

6. In bowl, combine cheeses. Spoon ⅓ of the cheeses over the noodles.

7. Repeat these layers twice.

8. Top with remaining meat sauce.

9. Cover and cook on Low for 4 hours.

Slow-Cooker Meat-Free Lasagna

**Rhonda Freed,
Lowville, NY**

Makes 6 servings
Prep. Time: 10 minutes
Cooking/Baking Time: 3–4 hours
Ideal slow-cooker size: 4-qt.

28-ounce jar spaghetti sauce, your choice of flavor
(or 3½ cups homemade, page 3)

6-7 lasagna noodles

2 cups shredded mozzarella cheese, divided

15 ounces ricotta cheese

¼ cup grated Parmesan cheese

1. Spread ¼ sauce in bottom of slow cooker.

2. Lay 2 noodles, broken into 1-inch pieces, over sauce.

3. In bowl, mix together 1½ cups mozzarella, ricotta, and Parmesan cheese.

4. Spoon ½ of cheese mixture onto noodles and spread out to edges.

5. Spoon in ⅓ of remaining sauce, and then 2 more broken noodles.

6. Spread remaining cheese mixture over top, then half the remaining sauce and all remaining noodles.

7. Finish with remaining sauce.

8. Cover and cook on Low for 3–4 hours, or until noodles are tender and cheeses are melted.

9. Add ½ cup mozzarella cheese and cook until cheese melts.

Lasagna Alfredo

Judy Buller,
Bluffton, OH

Makes 10–12 servings
Prep. Time: 30–45 minutes
Baking Time: 55–60 minutes
Standing Time: 15 minutes

9 lasagna noodles

½ cup chopped onion

1 garlic clove, minced

1 tablespoon olive oil

1 carrot, shredded

4 cups fresh, chopped spinach

1 cup chopped broccoli

¼ teaspoon salt

¼ teaspoon pepper

2 (15-ounce) jars Alfredo sauce or 3¾ cups
   homemade (page 12)

15-ounce carton ricotta cheese

½ cup Parmesan cheese

1 egg

2 cups shredded Colby or Monterey Jack cheese

1 cup shredded mozzarella cheese

1. Soak noodles in hot water for 15 minutes. Rinse, drain, and set aside.

2. In large skillet, cook onion and garlic in 1 tablespoon oil until crisp-tender. Add carrot, spinach, broccoli, salt, and pepper.

3. Remove ½ cup Alfredo sauce and set aside.

4. Stir remaining Alfredo sauce into skillet. Mix well and heat thoroughly. Set aside.

5. In large bowl, combine ricotta and Parmesan cheeses, egg, and Colby cheese. Mix well.

6. In greased 9×13-inch baking pan, spread ½ cup Alfredo sauce on bottom. Layer in this order: 3 noodles, ⅓ of cheese mixture, ⅓ of Alfredo sauce mixture.

7. Repeat layers two more times. Top with mozzarella cheese.

8. Cover and bake at 350°F for 45 minutes. Uncover and bake for 10 to 15 minutes more.

9. Let stand 15 minutes before serving.

Slow-Cooker Fresh Veggie Lasagna

Deanne Gingrich,
Lancaster, PA

Makes 4–6 servings
Prep. Time: 30 minutes
Cooking/Baking Time: 4 hours
Ideal slow-cooker size: 4- or 5-qt.

1½ cups shredded low-fat mozzarella cheese

½ cup low-fat ricotta cheese

⅓ cup grated Parmesan cheese

1 egg, lightly beaten

1 teaspoon dried oregano

¼ teaspoon garlic powder

24.5-ounce jar marinara pasta sauce, divided

1 medium zucchini, diced, divided

4 lasagna noodles

4 cups fresh baby spinach, divided

1 cup fresh mushrooms, sliced, divided

1. Grease interior of slow-cooker crock.

2. In bowl, mix together mozzarella, ricotta, and Parmesan cheeses, egg, oregano, and garlic powder. Set aside.

3. Spread ½ cup marinara sauce in crock.

4. Sprinkle with ½ the zucchini.

5. Spoon ⅓ of cheese mixture over zucchini.

6. Break two noodles into large pieces to cover cheese layer.

7. Spread ½ cup marinara over noodles.

8. Top with half the spinach and then half the mushrooms.

9. Repeat layers, ending with cheese mixture, and then sauce. Press layers down firmly.

10. Cover and cook on Low for 4 hours, or until vegetables are as tender as you like them and noodles are fully cooked.

11. Let stand for 15 minutes so lasagna can firm up before serving.

Creamy Baked Ziti

**Judi Manos,
West Islip, NY**

Makes 12 servings
Prep. Time: 20 minutes
Baking Time: 20 minutes

4 cups ziti

24.5-ounce jar marinara sauce

14.5-ounce can diced tomatoes

2 (3-ounce) packages cream cheese, cubed

¾ cup sour cream

8 ounces shredded mozzarella cheese, divided

⅓ cup freshly grated Parmesan cheese

1. Cook pasta as directed on package. Drain cooked pasta well.

2. While pasta drains, add marinara sauce, tomatoes and their juices, and cream cheese to cooking pot.

3. Cook on medium heat 5 minutes, or until cream cheese is melted and mixture is well blended. Stir frequently.

4. Return pasta to pan. Mix well.

5. Layer half the pasta mixture in greased 9×13-inch baking dish.

6. Cover with layer of sour cream.

7. Top with ½ of the mozzarella.

8. Spoon over remaining pasta mixture.

9. Top with remaining mozzarella.

10. Sprinkle with Parmesan cheese.

11. Bake 20 minutes, or until bubbly and heated through.

STOVETOP   OVEN

Turkey Tetrazzini

Carolyn Spohn,
Shawnee, KS

Makes 6–8 servings
Prep. Time: 30 minutes
Baking Time: 40 minutes

5 ounces spaghetti, broken

1 medium onion, chopped

1 medium green bell pepper, chopped

10.75-ounce can cream of chicken soup

⅓ cup milk

1 cup plain fat-free yogurt

3–4 cups diced cooked turkey

8-ounce can sliced ripe olives, drained

8-ounce can mushroom stems/pieces, drained

4-ounce jar chopped pimento, drained

Parmesan cheese, grated, optional

1 cup grated cheddar cheese

1. Cook spaghetti according to instructions on package. Drain well.

2. In nonstick skillet, sauté onion and bell pepper until soft.

3. In large mixing bowl, mix soup, milk, and yogurt together until smooth.

4. Stir into soup mixture the onion and bell pepper, spaghetti, turkey, olives, mushrooms, and pimento. Fold together until well mixed.

5. Pour into greased 9×13-inch baking dish.

6. Bake at 350°F for 30 minutes, or until bubbly.

7. Sprinkle with Parmesan cheese, if using. Then sprinkle with shredded cheddar cheese. Bake 10 more minutes.

TIP

This is a great recipe to use up leftover turkey from Thanksgiving!

Spaghetti Pie

Marlene Fonken,
Upland, CA

Makes 4 servings
Prep. Time: 15 minutes
Cooking/Baking Time: 45 minutes

4 ounces thin whole wheat spaghetti or vermicelli

1 tablespoon olive oil

2 tablespoons reduced-fat Parmesan cheese

2 egg whites, beaten

Nonstick cooking spray

⅔ cup cottage cheese or ½ cup ricotta

1 garlic clove, minced

½ cup diced onion

½ cup diced green or red bell sweet pepper

½ pound lean ground turkey

1 cup canned no-salt-added tomatoes, chopped,
    undrained

¼ cup tomato paste, no salt added

½ teaspoon dried basil

½ teaspoon dried oregano

¼ cup low-fat mozzarella cheese, shredded

1. Cook spaghetti according to instructions on package. Drain. Return to saucepan.

2. Stir oil, Parmesan cheese, and beaten egg whites into cooked spaghetti. Mix well.

3. Spray a glass 8-inch pie plate or 7×9-inch baking dish with nonstick cooking spray. Spread spaghetti mixture over bottom and up sides to form a crust.

4. Spread cottage cheese over bottom of crust.

5. In saucepan, cook garlic, onion, pepper, and turkey together until meat loses its pink color. (You may need to add a little water to pan to prevent sticking.)

6. Add tomatoes and their juices, tomato paste, basil, and oregano to pan. Cook until heated through.

7. Spoon turkey-tomato mixture over cottage cheese.

8. Bake, uncovered, for about 20 minutes at 350°F.

9. Sprinkle mozzarella cheese on top.

10. Continue to bake for another 5 minutes, or until cheese is melted.

Super Easy Pasta!

Chicken Noodle Casserole

Leesa DeMartyn
Enola, PA

Makes 6 servings
Prep. Time: 15–20 minutes
Baking Time: 30 minutes

8-ounce package egg noodles

1 tablespoon canola oil

¼ cup chopped onion

¼ cup chopped green bell pepper

2 cups cooked and cubed chicken

1 medium tomato, peeled and chopped

1 tablespoon lemon juice

¼ teaspoon salt

¼ teaspoon pepper

½ cup fat-free mayonnaise

⅓ cup fat-free milk

⅓ cup shredded reduced-fat cheddar cheese

Bread crumbs, optional

1. Cook egg noodles according to instructions on package. Drain and set aside.

2. In small skillet over medium heat, warm canola oil.

3. Sauté onion and bell pepper for about 5 minutes.

4. In large mixing bowl, combine sautéed vegetables with cooked noodles, chicken, tomato, lemon juice, salt, pepper, mayonnaise, and milk.

5. Turn into greased 2-quart casserole.

6. Top with cheese and with bread crumbs, if using.

7. Cover with foil. Bake at 400°F for 20 to 25 minutes, until heated through.

8. Let baked dish stand for 10 minutes before serving to allow sauce to thicken.

Slow-Cooker Tuna Noodle Casserole

**Leona Miller,
Millersburg, OH**

Makes 6 servings
Prep. Time: 20 minutes
Cooking/Baking Time: 3–9 hours
Ideal slow-cooker size: 4-qt.

2 (6.5-ounce) cans water-packed tuna, drained

2 (10.5-ounce) cans cream of mushroom soup

1 cup milk

2 tablespoons dried parsley

10-ounce package frozen mixed vegetables, thawed

8-ounce package noodles, cooked and drained

½ cup toasted sliced almonds

1. Combine tuna, soup, milk, parsley, and vegetables. Fold in noodles. Pour into greased slow cooker. Top with almonds.

2. Cover. Cook on Low for 7 to 9 hours, or High for 3 to 4 hours.

Spinach Cheese Manicotti

**Kimberly Richard,
Mars, PA**

Makes 7 servings
Prep. Time: 35 minutes
Baking Time: 45 minutes

15-ounce container ricotta cheese

10-ounce package frozen chopped spinach,
   thawed and squeezed dry

½ cup minced onion

¼ cup egg substitute

2 teaspoon parsley

½ teaspoon black pepper

½ teaspoon garlic powder

2 teaspoons dried basil

1¼ cups shredded mozzarella, divided

½ cup freshly grated Parmesan, divided

24.5-ounce jar marinara pasta sauce

1½ cups water

1 cup diced fresh tomatoes

8-ounce package manicotti shells

1. In large bowl, combine ricotta, spinach,
onion, and egg substitute.

2. Stir in parsley, black pepper, garlic powder,
and basil.

3. Mix in 1 cup mozzarella and ¼ cup
Parmesan cheese.

4. In separate bowl, mix together sauce, water,
and tomatoes.

5. Grease 9×13-inch baking pan. Spread 1 cup
spaghetti sauce in bottom of pan.

6. Stuff uncooked manicotti with ricotta
mixture. Arrange in single layer in baking pan.

7. Cover stuffed manicotti with remaining
sauce.

8. Sprinkle with remaining cheeses.

9. Cover. Bake at 350°F for 45 minutes, or until
bubbly.

Chicken Manicotti

Lori Showalter
New Hope, VA

Makes 4 servings
Serving size is 2 stuffed shells
Prep Time: 30 minutes
Baking Time: 65–70 minutes

¾ pound boneless, skinless chicken breasts

1½ teaspoons garlic powder

8 manicotti shells

26-ounce jar tomato and basil pasta sauce, divided

⅓ pound meatless, soy-based sausage, cooked and drained

¼ pound fresh mushrooms, sliced, or canned mushrooms, drained

1 cup (4 ounces) reduced-fat mozzarella cheese, shredded

⅓ cup water

1. Cut chicken into small chunks. In large bowl, toss chicken with garlic powder.

2. Stuff chicken into manicotti shells.

3. Spread 1 cup pasta sauce in bottom of greased 7x11-inch baking dish. Arrange stuffed shells on top of sauce.

4. Sprinkle with sausage and mushrooms. Pour remaining pasta sauce over top.

5. Sprinkle with cheese.

6. Spoon water around the edge of the dish. Cover and bake at 375°F for 65 to 70 minutes, or until chicken juices run clear and pasta is tender.

Garden Lasagna

Deb Martin,
Gap, PA

Makes 12 servings
Prep. Time: 30 minutes
Baking Time: 70–75 minutes

8 ounces lasagna noodles, divided

1-pound bag frozen broccoli, cauliflower, and carrots, divided

2 (10.75-ounce) cans cream of chicken soup

1 cup sour cream

¾ cup chicken broth

2 eggs or ½ cup egg substitute

3 cups cooked chopped chicken, divided

½ cup freshly grated Parmesan cheese, divided

1 cup mozzarella cheese, shredded

1. Cook noodles according to instructions on package. Drain well.

2. Steam vegetables until lightly cooked. Drain well.

3. In large bowl, mix soup, sour cream, broth, and eggs.

4. Place small amount of sauce on bottom of greased 9×13-inch baking pan. Swirl to cover bottom.

5. Layer 3 lasagna noodles on top of sauce.

6. Add ½ of soup mixture.

7. Top with ½ of chicken.

8. Top with ½ of vegetables.

9. Sprinkle with ½ of Parmesan cheese.

10. Repeat layers, using all remaining amounts of ingredients.

11. Top with mozzarella cheese.

12. Bake, covered, at 350°F for 1 hour.

13. Uncover. Bake another 10 to 15 minutes.

Meatless Lasagna Roll-Ups

Judy Buller,
Bluffton, OH

Makes 12 servings, 1 roll per serving
Prep. Time: 30 minutes
Baking Time: 25–30 minutes

12 lasagna noodles

2 eggs, slightly beaten

2½ cups ricotta cheese

2½ cups shredded mozzarella cheese, divided

½ cup freshly grated Parmesan cheese

1 package frozen, chopped spinach, thawed and squeezed dry, or 4 cups chopped fresh spinach that has been microwaved on High for 1 to 2 minutes and squeezed dry

¼ teaspoon salt

¼ teaspoon pepper

1–2 cups cooked black beans, rinsed and drained

24.5-ounce jar marinara pasta sauce, divided

1. Cook lasagna noodles in unsalted water according to instructions on package. Drain and rinse well. Lay flat.

2. In a large mixing bowl, mix together eggs, ricotta cheese, 1½ cups mozzarella cheese, Parmesan cheese, spinach, salt, and pepper.

3. Spread about ⅓ cup mixture on each noodle.

4. Sprinkle each noodle with black beans. Press down to make beans adhere.

5. Spread 1 cup marinara sauce in bottom of well greased 9×13-inch baking pan.

6. Roll up noodles and place seam-side down in baking pan.

7. Top rolls with remaining sauce. Sprinkle with 1 cup mozzarella cheese.

8. Bake uncovered at 350°F for 25 to 30 minutes, or until heated through.

Metric Equivalent Measurements

If you're accustomed to using metric measurements, I don't want you to be inconvenienced by the imperial measurements I use in this book.

You can also use this handy chart to figure out the size of the slow cooker you'll need for each recipe.

Weight (Dry Ingredients)

1 oz		30 g
4 oz	¼ lb	120 g
8 oz	½ lb	240 g
12 oz	¾ lb	360 g
16 oz	1 lb	480 g
32 oz	2 lb	960 g

Slow-Cooker Sizes

1-quart	0.96 l
2-quart	1.92 l
3-quart	2.88 l
4-quart	3.84 l
5-quart	4.80 l
6-quart	5.76 l
7-quart	6.72 l
8-quart	7.68 l

Volume (Liquid Ingredients)

½ tsp.		2 ml
1 tsp.		5 ml
1 Tbsp.	½ fl oz	15 ml
2 Tbsp.	1 fl oz	30 ml
¼ cup	2 fl oz	60 ml
⅓ cup	3 fl oz	80 ml
½ cup	4 fl oz	120 ml
⅔ cup	5 fl oz	160 ml
¾ cup	6 fl oz	180 ml
1 cup	8 fl oz	240 ml
1 pt	16 fl oz	480 ml
1 qt	32 fl oz	960 ml

Length

¼ in	6 mm
½ in	13 mm
¾ in	19 mm
1 in	25 mm
6 in	15 cm
12 in	30 cm

Index

Also Available